EVERY DAY COOKING FOR
DIABETES

75 quick and easy recipes
full of delicious ingredients
for a healthy diet bursting
with taste and goodness

EVERY DAY COOKING FOR
DIABETES

BRIDGET JONES

southwater

This edition is published by Southwater, an imprint of Anness Publishing Ltd, Hermes House, 88–89 Blackfriars Road, London SE1 8HA; tel. 020 7401 2077; fax 020 7633 9499

www.southwaterbooks.com; www.annesspublishing.com

If you like the images in this book and would like to investigate using them for publishing, promotions or advertising, please visit our website www.practicalpictures.com for more information.

UK agent: The Manning Partnership Ltd; tel. 01225 478444; fax 01225 478440;
sales@manning-partnership.co.uk
UK distributor: Book Trade Services; tel. 0116 2759086; fax 0116 2759090;
uksales@booktradeservices.com; exportsales@booktradeservices.com
North American agent/distributor: National Book Network; tel. 301 459 3366;
fax 301 429 5746; www.nbnbooks.com
Australian agent/distributor: Pan Macmillan Australia; tel. 1300 135 113;
fax 1300 135 103; customer.service@macmillan.com.au
New Zealand agent/distributor: David Bateman Ltd; tel. (09) 415 7664; fax (09) 415 8892

Publisher: Joanna Lorenz
Editorial Director: Helen Sudell
Executive Editor: Joanne Rippin
Photographs: Peter Anderson, Martin Brigdale, Nicky Dowey, Amanda Heywood, William Lingwood, Thomas Odulate, Craig Robertson, Simon Smith.
Recipes: Alex Barker, Michelle Beridale-Johnson, Georgina Campbell, Matthew Drennan, Joanna Farrow, Nicola Graimes, Becky Johnson, Maggie Mayhew, Keith Richmond, Rena Salaman, Jennie Shapter, Ysanne Spevack, Christopher Trotter, Kate Whiteman.
Production Controller: Christine Ni

ETHICAL TRADING POLICY
Because of our ongoing ecological investment programme, you, as our customer, can have the pleasure and reassurance of knowing that a tree is being cultivated on your behalf to naturally replace the materials used to make the book you are holding. For further information about this scheme, go to www.annesspublishing.com/trees.

PUBLISHER'S NOTE
Although the advice and information in this book are believed to be accurate and true at the time of going to press, neither the authors nor the publisher can accept any legal responsibility or liability for any errors or omissions that may be made nor for any inaccuracies nor for any harm or injury that comes about from following instructions or advice in this book.

NOTES
• Bracketed terms are intended for American readers.
• For all recipes, quantities are given in both metric and imperial measures and, where appropriate, in standard cups and spoons. Follow one set of measures, but not a mixture, because they are not interchangeable.
• Standard spoon and cup measures are level. 1 tsp = 5ml, 1 tbsp = 15ml, 1 cup = 250ml/8fl oz.
• Australian standard tablespoons are 20ml. Australian readers should use 3 tsp in place of 1 tbsp for measuring small quantities.
• American pints are 16fl oz/2 cups. American readers should use 20fl oz/ 2.5 cups in place of 1 pint when measuring liquids.
• Electric oven temperatures in this book are for conventional ovens. When using a fan oven, the temperature will probably need to be reduced by about 10–20°C/20–40°F. Since ovens vary, you should check with your manufacturer's instruction book for guidance.
• The nutritional analysis given for each recipe is calculated per portion (i.e. serving or item), unless otherwise stated. If the recipe gives a range, such as Serves 4–6, then the nutritional analysis will be for the smaller portion size, i.e. 6 servings. Measurements for sodium do not include salt added to taste.
• Medium (US large) eggs are used unless otherwise stated.

Contents

Introduction

Eating for long-term health is an important part of daily life for all of us; for people living with diabetes it is paramount. This is about being inclusive, not prohibitive, however; the more varied and interesting the diet, the better it is likely to be. Concentrate on beneficial ingredients and swing the balance away from foods that should be eaten in smaller proportions.

It is vital for anyone with diabetes to follow simple general guidelines for well-balanced eating, but no single eating pattern suits everyone, and getting a perspective on food means interpreting healthy diet information for your own lifestyle and taste.

Weight and diabetes

For good health, 'food in' has to equal 'energy out'. If you eat too much for your exercise levels, the excess is stored as fat, causing weight gain, and being overweight makes controlling diabetes difficult. Being overweight puts strain on organs and joints, and makes all activity harder than it should be. There is also a link between excess weight and insulin resistance.

Below: An active rather than sedentary lifestyle promotes a healthy appetite.

Above: Maintaining your ideal weight increases energy levels, and wellbeing.

Diet and exercise

In the management of diabetes, weight control, exercise and blood glucose control are all connected, so it is important to get advice from the dietician and follow it. Very low-calorie diets and exclusion diets that cut out whole food groups are not healthy, and are likely to interfere with blood glucose control. If the doctor and dietician recommend such a diet to reduce weight, it will be properly co-ordinated and managed, but this is not something to try unsupervised. Avoid faddy diets, meal substitutes and diet foods.

Follow the recommended proportions for different food groups, eating enough to supply your needs but not more. Regular exercise will help reduce weight and maintain a healthy weight in the long term.

Food in the right proportion

A daily intake of food, if not each meal, should consist of the following proportion of food types:
- A high proportion of starchy carbohydrates – 45–60 per cent of total calorific intake
- A high proportion of vegetables and fruit – at least 5 portions a day, but you should exceed this whenever possible
- A modest proportion of protein – about 10 per cent of total calories
- A small proportion of fat – less than 35 per cent of total calories (10–20 per cent of total calories should be from monounsaturated, less than 10 per cent from saturated, and less than 10 per cent from polyunsaturated fats)

Below: Healthy meals consist of the right proportions of each food type.

Above: Sugar has little nutritional value, whether it is white or brown.

• Limited foods containing sugar – up to 10% of the total calories, distributed throughout the day.

Drinks

Water is essential for all life, and the human body consists of about 70% water. We therefore need 2–3 litres/ 4½–7 pints every day. Raw vegetables and fruit contain a high percentage of water, and all drinks contribute to the intake, but it is important to drink water throughout the day. Stimulants such as tea and coffee should be kept to one or two cups a day, but fruit and herb teas are beneficial, as is green tea.

Carbonated drinks and too much fruit juice should be avoided because of the sugar levels. Alcohol does not have to be cut out completely, but should be limited and consumed with food.

Salt

Daily intake of salt should be less than 6g (⅕ oz). Most processed foods are over-salted, but in fresh food the nuances of flavour are lost when lots of salt is used. Getting into the habit of reducing salt in cooking will soon adjust your taste for salty foods downwards.

Fibre

While not a nutrient, fibre is vital for gut health, and especially helpful for diabetes as it helps to control blood glucose levels. Soluble fibre, the kind that is in oats, is helpful in lowering blood cholesterol and slows down the digestion of food. Insoluble fibre is the indigestible matter that absorbs water and passes through the gut. It slows down the rate at which food is digested and, because it absorbs moisture, is good for carrying away waste products.

Sugar and diabetes

There is lots of confusing information on sugar intake and blood glucose control, but whether you have diabetes or not, it is a good idea to limit your intake. It is not essential to exclude sugar entirely, but it should be limited to a small amount a day (about 25g/1oz) and this should be part of a dish, not sprinkled on food or stirred into drinks.

Sugar (sucrose) of any kind, syrups and honey add empty calories and have little food value. Eaten on their own, or in a high concentration, they cause blood glucose to rise high and quickly, causing fluctuations.

A moderate amount of sugary foods can be eaten when they are combined with other foods that help to slow down absorption. Artificial sweetners are an option, but it is better to develop a taste for unsweetened foods, and again they should only be used when combined with other foods.

GI values

Some carbohydrates are digested and absorbed more quickly than others, and it is these we should avoid or limit. The glycaemic index (GI) ranks carbohydrate absorption in comparison to glucose: on a scale of 0–100, glucose is rated at 100. Low GI foods are good, and high GI foods should be limited or balanced with low GI foods.

About the book

This book follows the contemporary approach to managing diabetes — to eat healthily, develop a taste for great food, and follow an inclusive diet. It offers lots of recipes to help you eat well and develop a positive approach to food, and has plenty of ideas from snacks and light meals to hearty family dinners with the occasional pudding that everyone can enjoy.

Above: Eating plenty of fruit, vegetables and wholegrain, slow-release carbohydrates will help keep energy levels high, and hunger satisfied.

Light meals and side dishes

To eat healthily, you need to manage your appetite; if you allow yourself to get too hungry before you eat you are likely to eat too much too quickly. It is also important to leave yourself enough time to prepare a nutritious snack or light meal, rather than reach for high-fat, high-calorie snacks that will satisfy you for only a short time and will give little nutritional value. The light meals and side dishes in this chapter can be prepared quickly, or made in advance and frozen. The soups are packed full of the best kinds of food, and can be frozen in individual portions, while the vegetable dishes and salads will complement any meat or fish dish.

Wild mushroom soup

Adding polenta to thin, but full-flavoured, soups is a great way of making a satisfying meal containing useful carbohydrate. Pasta shapes, macaroni, pearl barley or a mixture of wild rice and basmati rice are also good in soups, and offer the same benefits.

Serves six

20g/¾oz/scant ½ cup dried porcini
   mushrooms
175ml/6fl oz/¾ cup hot water
30ml/2 tbsp olive oil
1 large red onion, chopped
3 garlic cloves, chopped
115g/4oz/1¾ cups mixed wild
   mushrooms, trimmed
120ml/4fl oz/½ cup light red wine
1.2 litres/2 pints/5 cups vegetable stock
2.5ml/½ tsp wholegrain mustard
salt and ground black pepper
chopped fresh parsley, to garnish

For the polenta
750ml/1¼ pints/3 cups milk
175g/6oz/1 cup quick-cook polenta
50g/2oz/¼ cup butter
50g/2oz/⅔ cup freshly grated Parmesan
   cheese, plus extra to serve

1 Put the porcini in a bowl and pour over the hot water. Leave them to soak for about 30 minutes. Drain, and reserve the liquid and the mushrooms.

2 Heat the oil in a large pan. Add the onion and garlic and cook for 4–5 minutes. Add the wild mushrooms and cook for a further 3–4 minutes.

3 Add the dried mushrooms and strain in the soaking liquid through a muslin-lined sieve (strainer) or coffee filter. Pour in the wine and stock, and cook for 15 minutes or until reduced by half. Remove from the heat and cool slightly.

4 Ladle half the soup into a food processor or blender and process until almost smooth. Pour the processed soup back into the soup remaining in the pan and set aside.

5 To make the polenta, bring the milk to the boil and pour in the polenta in a steady stream, stirring continuously. Cook for about 5 minutes, or until the polenta begins to come away from the side of the pan. Beat in the butter, then stir in the Parmesan.

6 Return the soup to the heat and bring just to the boil. Stir in the wholegrain mustard and season well.

7 Divide the polenta among six bowls and ladle the soup around it. Sprinkle with grated Parmesan and parsley.

Cook's tip
Many supermarkets now sell a range of wild mushrooms. If you can't find fresh wild mushrooms, then substitute a mixture of cultivated varieties, such as shiitake and brown cap (cremini).

Energy 149kcal/618kJ; Protein 3.1g; Carbohydrate 9g, of which sugars 0.5g; Fat 11.4g, of which saturates 6.9g; Cholesterol 28mg; Calcium 25mg; Fibre 1.5g; Sodium 79mg.

Butter bean and sun-dried tomato soup

This soup is easy to make for a quick lunch or supper. The key is to use a flavoursome fresh stock, whether home-made or store-bought, with good-quality pesto and sun-dried tomato purée. Follow on with a couple of pieces of fresh fruit for dessert.

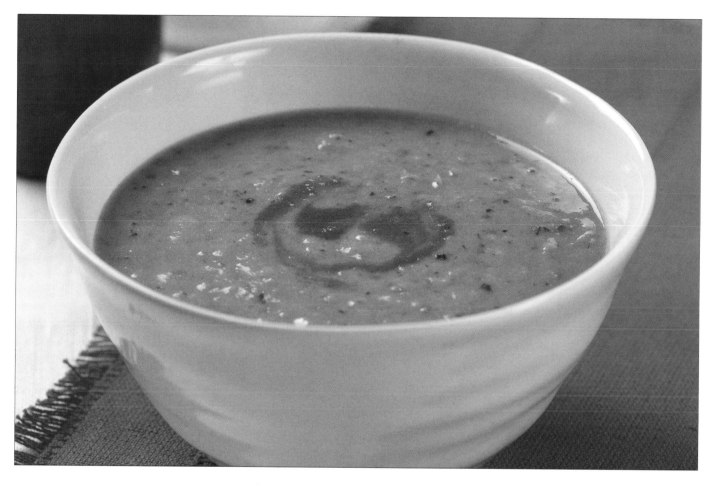

Serves four

2 x 400g/14oz cans butter (lima) beans,
   drained and rinsed
900ml/1½ pints/3¾ cups chicken
   or vegetable stock
60ml/4 tbsp sun-dried tomato purée (paste)
75ml/5 tbsp pesto

Cook's tips
Try using chickpeas instead of butter beans, omit the sun-dried tomato purée (paste) and add chopped fresh parsley, spring onions (scallions) or chives, and finely grated lemon rind. Process all the soup for a smoother texture. Swirl yogurt into the soup to serve.

1 Put the butter beans in a pan. Pour in the stock and stir well. Bring the beans to the boil over a medium heat, stirring once or twice.

2 Stir in the tomato purée and pesto. Lower the heat and cover, and cook gently for 5 minutes.

3 Transfer six ladlefuls of the soup to a blender or food processor, scooping up plenty of the beans. Process until smooth, then return to the pan.

4 Heat gently, stirring frequently, for 5 minutes, then season if necessary. Ladle into four warmed soup bowls and serve with warm crusty bread or breadsticks.

Energy 269kcal/1130kJ; Protein 15.6g; Carbohydrate 28.3g, of which sugars 4.5g; Fat 11.2g, of which saturates 2.5g; Cholesterol 6mg; Calcium 111mg; Fibre 9.7g; Sodium 944mg.

Roasted pumpkin soup

Chinese medicine prescribes pumpkin for diabetes, and recent studies have indicated that there could be properties in the vegetable that may increase insulin levels. Whether or not this is verified, pumpkin is ideal as the basis for a healthy, slow-release carboydrate meal.

Serves six to eight

1.5kg/3–3½lb pumpkin
30ml/2 tbsp olive oil
2 onions, chopped
3 garlic cloves, chopped
7.5cm/3in piece fresh root ginger, grated
5ml/1 tsp ground coriander
2.5ml/½ tsp ground turmeric
pinch of cayenne pepper
1 litre/1¾ pints/4 cups vegetable stock
salt and ground black pepper
15ml/1 tbsp sesame seeds and
  fresh coriander leaves, to garnish

For the pumpkin crisps
wedge of fresh pumpkin, seeded
120ml/4fl oz/½ cup olive oil

1 Preheat the oven to 200°C/400°F/ Gas 6. Prick the pumpkin around the top several times with a fork.

2 Bake the whole pumpkin in the hot oven for 45 minutes or until tender. Leave until cool enough to handle.

3 When the pumpkin has cooled sufficiently, cut it in half and scrape off and discard the seeds. Take care when cutting the pumpkin as there may still be a lot of hot steam inside.

4 Cut the pumpkin flesh into slices, and then into chunks, discarding the skin. Set aside.

5 Heat the oil (you may not have to use all of it) in a large pan and add the onions, garlic and ginger, then cook gently for 4–5 minutes.

6 Add the coriander, turmeric and cayenne, and cook for 2 minutes. Stir in the pumpkin flesh and stock. Bring to the boil, reduce the heat and simmer for 20 minutes.

7 Cool the soup slightly, then purée it in a food processor or blender until smooth. Return the soup to the rinsed-out pan and season well.

8 Meanwhile, prepare the pumpkin crisps. Using a swivel-blade potato peeler, pare long thin strips off the wedge of pumpkin.

EAT WELL
Serve the fried pumpkin crisps on special occasions; for everyday, slow-release carbohydrate, top the soup with chunky wholemeal croûtons and pumpkin seeds.
  Lightly brush thick slices of stoneground wholemeal (whole-wheat) bread with olive oil, cut them into small pieces, spread in a single layer on a baking tray, and in a medium oven bake until crisp and brown, sprinkle with unsalted pumpkin seeds about halfway through cooking.

9 Heat the oil in a small saucepan and fry the strips in batches for 2 minutes, until crisp. Drain on kitchen paper.

10 Reheat the soup and ladle it into bowls. Top with the pumpkin crisps and garnish each portion with sesame seeds and coriander leaves.

Cook's tip
If only very large pumpkins are available, simply cut off two or three large wedges weighing 1.5kg/3–3½lb in total. Roast the wedges as above for 20–30 minutes or until tender.

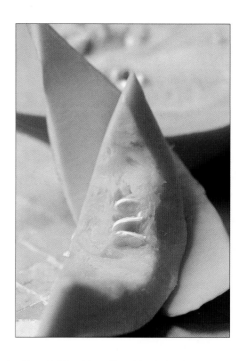

Energy 203kcal/839kJ; Protein 2.3g; Carbohydrate 8.3g, of which sugars 6.2g; Fat 18.1g, of which saturates 2.7g; Cholesterol 0mg; Calcium 82mg; Fibre 2.8g; Sodium 2mg.

Golden chorizo and chickpea soup

The advantage of using highly flavoured sausages is that a small amount goes a long way, keeping the fat content under control. The bulk of this recipe comes from valuable low-GI chickpeas, and new potatoes – which have a lower GI count than mature potatoes.

Cook's tip
For a low-fat version, cook diced skinless, boneless chicken in the minimum of olive oil instead of the chorizo sausage.

3 Add the chilli flakes and garlic to the fat in the pan, stir through and cook for a few seconds.

4 Stir in the saffron with its soaking water, tomatoes, chickpeas, potatoes, chorizo sausages and bay leaves.

5 Pour 450ml/¾ pint/scant 2 cups of the chickpea cooking liquid into the pan, add the water, and stir in salt and pepper to taste.

6 Bring to the boil, then reduce the heat and simmer for 45–50 minutes, stirring gently occasionally, until the potatoes are tender and the soup has thickened slightly.

7 Add the chopped parsley to the soup and adjust the seasoning. Ladle the soup into four large, warmed soup plates. Serve with crusty bread.

Serves four

115g/4oz/⅔ cup dried chickpeas, soaked overnight and drained
pinch of saffron strands
45ml/3 tbsp olive oil
225g/8oz uncooked mini chorizo sausages
5ml/1 tsp dried chilli flakes
6 garlic cloves, finely chopped
450g/1lb tomatoes, roughly chopped
350g/12oz new potatoes, quartered
2 bay leaves
450ml/¾ pint/scant 2 cups water
60ml/4 tbsp chopped fresh parsley
salt and ground black pepper
crusty bread, to serve

1 Place the chickpeas in a large pan. Cover with fresh water and bring to the boil, skimming off any scum as it forms. Cover and simmer for about 1½ hours, until tender. Add more water, if necessary, to keep the chick-peas covered during cooking. Drain, reserving the cooking liquid. Soak the saffron strands in a little warm water.

2 Heat the oil in a large, deep frying pan. Add the chorizo sausages and fry over a medium heat for 5 minutes, until a lot of oil has seeped out of the sausages and they are pale golden brown. Drain and set aside.

Energy 642kcal/2674kJ; Protein 21.7g; Carbohydrate 42.3g, of which sugars 8.1g; Fat 44g, of which saturates 12.5g; Cholesterol 68mg; Calcium 174mg; Fibre 6.1g; Sodium 997mg.

Scotch broth

Sustaining and warming, Scotch broth is custom-made for damp, chilly weather, and makes a delicious winter soup anywhere. This version has added pearl barley for extra slow-release carbohydrate, which is added at the end so it tastes nutty and wholesome.

Serves six to eight

1kg/2¼lb lean neck (US shoulder or breast) of lamb, cut into large, even chunks

1.75 litres/3 pints/7½ cups cold water

1 large onion, chopped

175g/6oz/¾ cup pearl barley

bouquet garni

1 large carrot, chopped

1 turnip, chopped

3 leeks, chopped

1 small white cabbage, finely shredded

salt and ground black pepper

chopped fresh parsley, to garnish

1 Put the lamb and water in a large pan over a medium heat and gently bring to the boil. Skim off the scum with a spoon. Add the onion, half the barley and bouquet garni, and mix thoroughly.

2 Bring the soup back to the boil, then reduce the heat, partly cover the pan and simmer for a further 1 hour. Make sure that it does not boil too fast.

3 Add the remaining vegetables and barley to the pan and season with salt and ground black pepper. Bring to the boil, partly cover again and simmer for about 35 minutes, until the vegetables are tender.

4 When the soup is cooked, remove the surplus fat that will have collected on the surface with a sheet of kitchen paper. Serve the soup hot, garnished with chopped parsley, with chunks of fresh bread.

Energy 290kcal/1214kJ; Protein 27.1g; Carbohydrate 13.3g, of which sugars 6.8g; Fat 14.6g, of which saturates 6.6g; Cholesterol 95mg; Calcium 65mg; Fibre 3.3g; Sodium 118mg.

Ribollita

With lots of vegetables and beans, this classic soup makes a healthy meal full of vitamins, slow-release carbohydrate and fibre. Vary the vegetables depending on what is available.

Serves four

115g/4oz/generous ½ cup dried cannellini
    beans, soaked overnight and drained
8 garlic cloves, unpeeled
30ml/2 tbsp olive oil
6 celery sticks, chopped
3 carrots, chopped
2 onions, chopped
400g/14oz can plum tomatoes, drained
30ml/2 tbsp chopped fresh flat leaf parsley
grated rind and juice of 1 lemon
800g/1¾lb cavolo nero cabbage, sliced
1 day-old ciabatta loaf
salt and ground black pepper
olive oil, to serve

1 Put the beans in a pan and cover with fresh water. Bring to the boil and boil for 10 minutes. Drain again. Cover generously with fresh cold water and add six garlic cloves. Bring to the boil, cover and simmer for 45–60 minutes, until the beans are tender. (The cooking time varies according to how old the beans are.) Set the beans aside in their cooking liquid.

2 Heat the oil in a pan. Peel and chop the remaining garlic and add it to the pan with the celery, carrots and onions. Cook gently for 10 minutes, until beginning to soften.

3 Stir in the tomatoes, parsley, lemon rind and juice. Cover and simmer for 25 minutes. Add the sliced cavolo nero cabbage and half the cannellini beans with enough of their cooking liquid to cover all of the ingredients. Simmer for 30 minutes.

4 Process the remaining beans with a little of their remaining cooking liquid in a food processor or blender until just smooth. Add to the pan and pour in boiling water to thin the mixture to the consistency of a thick soup.

5 Remove the crust from the ciabatta and tear the bread into rough pieces, then stir them into the soup. Season well. This soup should be very thick, but you may need to add a little more boiling water. Ladle the soup into bowls and drizzle over a little olive oil.

Energy 104kcal/436kJ; Protein 5.7g; Carbohydrate 14.5g, of which sugars 6.9g; Fat 3g, of which saturates 0.5g; Cholesterol 0mg; Calcium 78mg; Fibre 5.9g; Sodium 218mg.

Bean and pistou soup

This hearty soup makes an excellent vegetarian meal, with a good mix of carbohydrate and green vegetables. Round off the food value by having fresh fruit to follow.

Serves four to six

150g/5oz/scant 1 cup dried haricot (navy) beans, soaked overnight in cold water
150g/5oz/scant 1 cup dried flageolet or cannellini beans, soaked overnight in cold water
1 onion, chopped
1.2 litres/2 pints/5 cups hot vegetable stock
2 carrots, roughly chopped
225g/8oz Savoy cabbage, shredded
1 large potato, about 225g/8oz, roughly chopped
225g/8oz French (green) beans, chopped
salt and ground black pepper
basil leaves, to garnish

For the pistou
4 garlic cloves
8 large sprigs basil leaves
90ml/6 tbsp olive oil
60ml/4 tbsp freshly grated Parmesan cheese

1 Drain the soaked haricot and flageolet or cannellini beans and place in a casserole pot. Add the chopped onion and pour over sufficient cold water to come 5cm/2in above the beans. Cover and place the pot in an unheated oven. Set the oven to 200°C/400°F/Gas 6 and cook for about 1½ hours, or until the beans are tender.

2 Drain the beans and onions. Place half the beans and onions in a food processor or blender and process to a paste. Return the drained beans and the bean paste to the casserole pot. Add the hot vegetable stock.

3 Add the chopped carrots, shredded cabbage, chopped potato and French beans to the pot. Season with salt and pepper, cover and return the pot to the oven. Reduce the oven temperature to 180°C/350°F/Gas 4 and cook for about 1 hour, or until all the vegetables are cooked right through.

4 Meanwhile, place the garlic and basil in a mortar and pound with a pestle, then gradually beat in the oil. Stir in the grated Parmesan. Stir half the pistou into the soup and then ladle into warmed soup bowls. Top each bowl of soup with a spoonful of the remaining pistou and serve garnished with basil.

Energy 332kcal/1392kJ; Protein 17.1g; Carbohydrate 33.3g, of which sugars 6.2g; Fat 15.4g, of which saturates 3.8g; Cholesterol 10mg; Calcium 211mg; Fibre 10.4g; Sodium 129mg.

American red bean soup with salsa

Avocados are one of the best sources of monounsaturated fat, which lowers artery-clogging LDL cholesterol and raises heart-healthy HDL cholesterol, so it is recommended for diabetics.

3 Bring the tomato and bean mixture to the boil and simmer for 15–20 minutes. Cool the soup slightly, then purée it in a food processor or blender until smooth. Return to the rinsed-out pan and add seasoning to taste.

4 To make the guacamole salsa, halve, stone (pit) and peel the avocados, then dice them finely. Place in a small bowl and gently, but thoroughly, mix with the finely chopped red onion and chilli, and the coriander and lime juice.

5 Reheat the soup and ladle into bowls. Spoon a little guacamole salsa into the middle of each and serve, offering Tabasco sauce for those who want to spice up their soup.

Serves six

30ml/2 tbsp olive oil
2 onions, chopped
2 garlic cloves, chopped
10ml/2 tsp ground cumin
1.5ml/¼ tsp cayenne pepper
15ml/1 tbsp paprika
15ml/1 tbsp tomato purée (paste)
2.5ml/½ tsp dried oregano
400g/14oz can chopped tomatoes
2 x 400g/14oz cans red kidney beans,
   drained and rinsed
900ml/1½ pints/3¾ cups water
salt and ground black pepper
Tabasco sauce, to serve

For the guacamole salsa
2 avocados
1 small red onion, finely chopped
1 green chilli, seeded and finely chopped
15ml/1 tbsp chopped fresh coriander (cilantro)
juice of 1 lime

1 Heat the oil in a large, heavy-based pan and add the onions and garlic. Cook for about 4–5 minutes, until softened. Add the cumin, cayenne and paprika, and cook for 1 minute, stirring continuously.

2 Stir in the tomato purée and cook for a few seconds, then stir in the oregano. Add the chopped tomatoes, kidney beans and water.

> **EAT WELL**
> This is the sort of soup to make in a big batch and freeze in small portions ready to thaw in the microwave for an instant lunch or supper. Instead of salsa, the reheated soup can be topped with a poached egg and strips of quickly sautéed red (bell) pepper.

Energy 254kcal/1064kJ; Protein 10.8g; Carbohydrate 29.2g, of which sugars 9.1g; Fat 11.2g, of which saturates 2.1g; Cholesterol 0mg; Calcium 111mg; Fibre 10.6g; Sodium 535mg.

Cod, broad bean and spinach chowder

Fresh cod and vegetables are abundant in this hearty, nutritionally balanced soup. Spinach is packed with nutrients, and is thought to help prevent diabetes from developing.

Serves six

1 litre/2 pints/4 cups milk
675g/1¼lb cod fillet, skinned and boned
30ml/2 tbsp olive oil
1 onion, sliced
2 garlic cloves, finely chopped
750g/1½lb potatoes, thickly sliced
450g/1lb fresh broad (fava) beans, podded
450g/1lb baby spinach leaves
pinch of freshly grated nutmeg
30ml/2 tbsp chopped fresh chives
salt and ground black pepper
fresh chives, to garnish

For the Granary croûtons
60ml/4 tbsp olive oil
6 slices Granary (whole-wheat) bread, crusts
   removed and cut into large cubes

1 Pour the milk into a large pan and bring to the boil. Add the cod and simmer gently for 2 minutes, then remove from the heat and leave to stand for about 6 minutes, until the fish is just cooked. Use a slotted spoon to remove the fish from the cooking liquid.

2 Using a fork, flake the cooked cod into chunky pieces, removing bones or skin, then cover and set aside.

3 Heat the olive oil in a large pan and add the onion and garlic. Cook for about 5 minutes, until softened, stirring occasionally. Add the potatoes, stir in the milk and bring to the boil. Reduce the heat and cover the pan. Cook for 10 minutes. Add the broad beans; cook for 10 minutes more or until the beans are tender and the potatoes just begin to break up.

Cook's tip
When broad (fava) beans are out of season, frozen beans are a good alternative: cook them for 5 minutes.

4 Meanwhile, to make the croûtons, heat the oil in a frying pan and add the bread cubes. Cook over a medium heat, stirring often, until golden all over. Remove using a draining spoon and leave to drain on kitchen paper.

5 Add the pieces of cod to the soup and heat through gently.

6 Just before serving, add the spinach and stir for 1–2 minutes, until wilted. Season the soup well and stir in the nutmeg and chives.

7 Ladle the soup into six warmed soup bowls and scatter some croûtons on top of each. Garnish with fresh chives and serve at once.

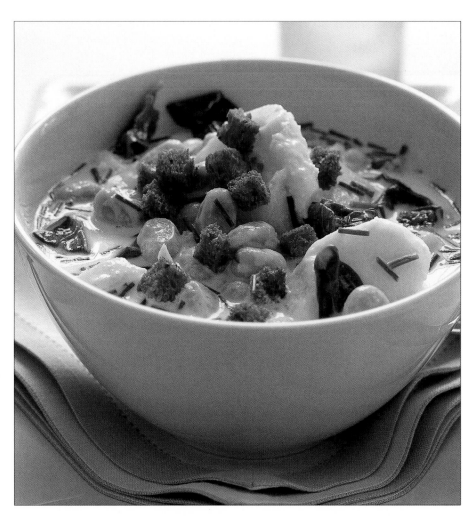

Energy 502kcal/2110kJ; Protein 39.3g; Carbohydrate 51.6g, of which sugars 12.9g; Fat 16.7g, of which saturates 3.9g; Cholesterol 62mg; Calcium 452mg; Fibre 8.8g; Sodium 427mg.

Caribbean salt cod soup with yam

This colourful chunky soup is inspired by the ingredients of the Caribbean. Yam has a low GI rating, and so makes a good carbohydrate element to a balanced meal.

3 Stir in the tomatoes, wine and bay leaves and bring to the boil. Pour in the water, bring to the boil, reduce the heat and simmer for 10 minutes.

4 Meanwhile, trim the stalk ends off the okra and cut the pods into chunks. Add to the soup and cook for 10 minutes. Stir in the callaloo or spinach and cook for 5 minutes, until the okra is tender.

5 Meanwhile, prepare the creamed yam. Peel the yam and cut it into large dice, then place in a pan with the lemon juice and add cold water to cover. Bring to the boil and cook for 15–20 minutes, until tender.

6 Drain the yam, then return to the pan and dry it over the heat for a few seconds. Mash with the oil and yogurt, and season well. Stir in the chives.

7 Season the soup and stir in the chopped parsley. Spoon portions of creamed yam into the centres of six soup bowls and ladle the soup around it. Serve immediately.

Serves six

200g/7oz salt cod, soaked for 24 hours
15ml/1 tbsp olive oil
1 garlic clove, chopped
1 onion, chopped
1 green chilli, seeded and chopped
6 plum tomatoes, peeled and chopped
250ml/8fl oz/1 cup white wine
2 bay leaves
900ml/1½ pints/3¾ cups water
225g/8oz okra
225g/8oz callaloo or spinach
30ml/2 tbsp chopped fresh parsley
salt and ground black pepper

For the creamed yam
675g/1½lb yam
juice of 1 lemon
30ml/2 tbsp olive oil
30ml/2 tbsp low-fat Greek (US strained plain) yogurt
15ml/1 tbsp chopped fresh chives

1 While the cod is soaking you will need to change the water several times. Drain and skin the salt cod, then rinse it under cold running water. Cut into bitesize pieces, removing any bones, and set aside.

2 Heat the oil in a heavy pan. Add the garlic, onion and chilli, and cook for 4–5 minutes until softened. Add the salt cod and cook for 3–4 minutes, until it begins to colour.

EAT WELL
Mashing yam speeds up the rate at which it is digested (just like potatoes) but eating it as part of a meal (with protein from fish) slows down the process. Low-fat Greek yogurt gives a creamy texture, and olive oil adds flavour.

Energy 322kcal/1352kJ; Protein 10.7g; Carbohydrate 36.7g, of which sugars 5.3g; Fat 12.8g, of which saturates 6.6g; Cholesterol 40mg; Calcium 159mg; Fibre 4.6g; Sodium 137mg.

Moroccan chicken soup

Infused with the pungent flavours of North Africa, this spiced soup is served with a rich and tangy lemon butter. Including protein means that the soup will keep you satisfied for longer.

Serves six

50g/2oz/¼ cup butter
450g/1lb skinless boneless chicken breasts,
    cut into strips
1 onion, chopped
2 garlic cloves, crushed
7.5ml/1½ tsp plain (all-purpose) flour
15ml/1 tbsp harissa
1 litre/1¾ pints/4 cups chicken stock
400g/14oz can chopped tomatoes
400g/14oz can chickpeas, drained and rinsed
salt and ground black pepper
lemon wedges, to serve

For the charmoula
50g/2oz/¼ cup slightly salted butter,
    at room temperature
30ml/2 tbsp chopped fresh coriander (cilantro)
2 garlic cloves, crushed
5ml/1 tsp ground cumin
1 red chilli, seeded and chopped
pinch of saffron strands
finely grated rind of ½ lemon
5ml/1 tsp paprika
25g/1oz/1 cup dried breadcrumbs

1 Melt the butter in a large, heavy pan. Add the chicken strips and cook for 5–6 minutes, until beginning to brown.

2 Use a slotted spoon to remove it from the pan and set aside. Add the onion and garlic and cook over a gentle heat for 4–5 minutes, until softened.

3 Stir in the flour and cook for 3–4 minutes, stirring, until beginning to brown. Stir in the harissa and cook for a further 1 minute.

4 Gradually pour in the stock and cook for 2–3 minutes, until slightly thickened. Stir in the tomatoes.

5 Return the chicken to the soup and add the chickpeas. Cover and cook over a low heat for 20 minutes. Season well.

6 Meanwhile, to make the charmoula, put the butter into a bowl and beat in the coriander, garlic, cumin, chilli, saffron strands, lemon rind and paprika. When the mixture is well combined, stir in the coarse breadcrumbs.

7 Ladle the soup into warmed bowls. Spoon a little of the charmoula into the centre of each and leave for a few seconds to allow the butter to melt into the soup before serving with lemon wedges.

Energy 313kcal/1312kJ; Protein 25g; Carbohydrate 18.3g, of which sugars 3.3g; Fat 16.1g, of which saturates 9g; Cholesterol 88mg; Calcium 53mg; Fibre 3.6g; Sodium 207mg.

Braised red cabbage

Red cabbage is full of anthocyanins, which are thought to help protect against heart disease. It is ideal for mixing with robust spices and flavourings. Traditionally served as an accompaniment to roast pork, duck and game dishes, it also goes well with fish dishes.

3 Layer the shredded cabbage in a large ovenproof dish with the onions, apples, spices, and salt and ground black pepper. Pour over the vinegar and walnut oil.

4 Cover the dish with a lid and cook in the preheated oven for about 1½ hours, stirring a couple of times, until the cabbage is very tender. Serve immediately, garnished with the parsley.

Serves four to six

1kg/2¼lb red cabbage
2 cooking apples
2 onions, chopped
1.5ml/¼ tsp freshly grated nutmeg
pinch of ground cloves
1.5ml/¼ tsp ground cinnamon
15ml/1 tbsp red wine vinegar
30ml/2 tbsp walnut oil
salt and ground black pepper
chopped flat leaf parsley, to garnish

1 Preheat the oven to 160°C/325°F/ Gas 3.

2 Cut away and discard the large white ribs from the outer cabbage leaves using a large, sharp knife, then finely shred the cabbage. Peel, core and coarsely grate the apples.

Energy 160kcal/668kJ; Protein 4.3g; Carbohydrate 23.8g, of which sugars 22.4g; Fat 5.8g, of which saturates 3.3g; Cholesterol 13mg; Calcium 140mg; Fibre 6.6g; Sodium 58mg.

Kale with mustard dressing

Sea kale's pale green fronds have a slightly nutty taste, and can be eaten raw. Use curly kale or a dark green cabbage if you can't get sea kale, but you will need to boil it for a few minutes before dressing and serving. All leafy greens are packed full of vitamins and minerals.

Serves four

250g/9oz sea kale or curly kale
45ml/3 tbsp light olive oil
5ml/1 tsp wholegrain mustard
15ml/1 tbsp white wine vinegar
pinch of caster (superfine) sugar
salt and ground black pepper

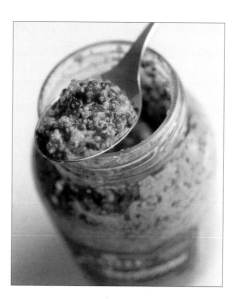

1 Wash the kale, drain, then trim it and tear in pieces. Cook briefly if needed.

2 Whisk the oil into the mustard in a bowl. When it is blended completely, whisk in the white wine vinegar. It should begin to thicken.

3 Season the mustard dressing to taste with sugar, a little salt and plenty of ground black pepper.

4 Toss the sea kale in the dressing and serve immediately.

Energy 99kcal/409kJ; Protein 2.1g; Carbohydrate 1.9g, of which sugars 1.9g; Fat 9.3g, of which saturates 1.3g; Cholesterol 0mg; Calcium 82mg; Fibre 1.9g; Sodium 27mg.

Broccoli with sesame seeds

Quick cooking is best for tender young purple-sprouting broccoli, so that the rich colour and crunchy texture is retained. A splash of soy sauce and some toasted sesame seeds complement the flavour of this supremely healthy vegetable.

Serves two

225g/8oz purple-sprouting broccoli
15ml/1 tbsp sesame seeds
15ml/1 tbsp olive oil
15ml/1 tbsp soy sauce
salt and ground black pepper

EAT WELL

When purple-sprouting broccoli is not available, remove the stalks from ordinary broccoli and dice them, then blanch them in boiling water for 2–3 minutes before stirring with the broccoli tops. For a healthy lunch, make a double portion and serve it with couscous, topped with chopped walnuts or pine nuts.

1 Using a sharp knife, cut off and discard any thick stems from the broccoli and cut the broccoli into long, thin florets.

2 Spread out the sesame seeds in a small frying pan and dry-fry over a medium heat until toasted. Shake the pan occasionally and do not leave them unattended as the seeds will readily burn if left just a fraction too long.

3 Heat the olive oil in a wok or large frying pan and add the broccoli. Stir-fry for 3–4 minutes, or until tender, adding a splash of water if the pan becomes too dry.

4 Add the soy sauce to the broccoli, then season with salt and ground black pepper to taste. Add the toasted sesame seeds, toss to combine and serve immediately.

Energy 270kcal/1115kJ; Protein 13.1g; Carbohydrate 5.4g, of which sugars 4.6g; Fat 21.7g, of which saturates 3.3g; Cholesterol 0mg; Calcium 229mg; Fibre 7.1g; Sodium 1089mg.

Young vegetables with tarragon

This is almost a salad, but the vegetables here are just lightly cooked to bring out their different flavours. The tarragon adds a wonderful depth to this bright, fresh dish. Broccoli, cauliflower or Brussels sprouts are also good cooked this way.

Serves four

5 spring onions (scallions)
30ml/2 tbsp olive oil
1 garlic clove, crushed
115g/4oz asparagus tips
115g/4oz mangetouts (snow peas), trimmed
115g/4oz broad (fava) beans
2 Little Gem (Bibb) lettuces
5ml/1 tsp finely chopped fresh tarragon
salt and ground black pepper

Cook's tip

For a main course, serve the vegetables with wholemeal (whole-wheat) pasta, topped with low-fat fromage frais and Parmesan shavings.

1 Cut the spring onions into quarters lengthways and fry them gently over a medium-low heat in the oil with the garlic.

2 Add the asparagus tips, mangetouts and broad beans to the frying pan. Mix in well with the oil, and add enough water to just cover the base of the pan.

3 Bring the vegetables to the boil, and then reduce the heat. Allow to simmer for 5–8 minutes, until the vegetables are starting to soften but not overcooked.

4 Cut the lettuce into quarters and add to the pan. Cook for 3 minutes then, off the heat, add the tarragon, and serve.

Energy 124kcal/515kJ; Protein 5.1g; Carbohydrate 6.8g, of which sugars 3.5g; Fat 8.7g, of which saturates 3.8g; Cholesterol 13mg; Calcium 62mg; Fibre 3.9g; Sodium 44mg.

Courgettes in tomato sauce

This rich-flavoured dish can be served hot or cold, as a base for grilled gammon or griddled tofu, or with plain roast chicken. Cut the courgettes into fairly thick slices, so that they retain their texture and stay slightly crunchy.

Serves four

15ml/1 tbsp olive oil
1 onion, chopped
1 garlic clove, chopped
4 courgettes (zucchini), thickly sliced
400g/14oz can chopped tomatoes
2 tomatoes, peeled, seeded and chopped
15ml/1 tbsp tomato purée (paste)
salt and ground black pepper

EAT WELL
Add two sliced, seeded red (bell) peppers with the courgettes in step 1 and serve in baked potatoes, with poached eggs.

---

1 Heat the olive oil in a heavy pan, add the chopped onion and garlic and sauté for about 5 minutes, or until the onion is softened, stirring occasionally.

2 Add the thickly sliced courgettes to the onion and garlic and cook for a further 5 minutes.

3 Add the canned and fresh tomatoes, and tomato purée to the pan, and stir together. Simmer for 10–15 minutes until the sauce is thickened and the courgettes are tender. If the sauce becomes too dry, add a little water. Season to taste and serve.

Baked fennel with a crumb crust

Baked fennel is tasty and versatile – good with classic roasts or all kinds of dishes, from pasta and risotto to pizza or tortilla. This crunchy breadcrumb topping complements it perfectly.

Serves four

4 fennel bulbs, cut lengthwise into quarters
1 garlic clove, chopped
75g/3oz/1½ cups day-old wholemeal (whole-wheat) breadcrumbs
45ml/3 tbsp chopped fresh flat leaf parsley
30ml/2 tbsp olive oil
salt and ground black pepper
a few fronds of fennel leaves, to garnish (optional)

EAT WELL
Vegetables with good flavour and texture, such as fennel, are excellent with tofu or bean curd. For a delicious main dish, cut a couple of packets of firm tofu into thick fingers and arrange them in the dish with the fennel.

---

1 Cook the fennel in a pan of boiling salted water for 10 minutes. Preheat the oven to 190°C/375°F/Gas 5. Drain the fennel and place in a large ovenproof dish.

2 In a small bowl, mix together the chopped garlic, wholemeal breadcrumbs and chopped fresh flat leaf parsley, then stir half of the olive oil.

3 Brush the fennel with the rest of the olive oil. Sprinkle the breadcrumb mixture evenly over the top, then season well with salt and pepper. Place the dish in the hot oven.

4 Bake the fennel for about 30 minutes, or until it is tender and the breadcrumb topping is crisp and golden brown. Serve the baked fennel hot, garnished with a few fronds of fennel leaves, if you like.

Energy 89kcal/370kJ; Protein 4.3g; Carbohydrate 9.2g, of which sugars 8.6g; Fat 4.1g, of which saturates 0.7g; Cholesterol 0mg; Calcium 54mg; Fibre 3.2g; Sodium 235mg.
Energy 114kcal/477kJ; Protein 3g; Carbohydrate 12.6g, of which sugars 3.1g; Fat 6.1g, of which saturates 0.8g; Cholesterol 0mg; Calcium 67mg; Fibre 4.3g; Sodium 114mg.

Lentil dhal with roasted garlic and spices

This is an incredibly simple and tasty curry which is also for people with diabetes. It's low in fat and provides plenty of starchy carbohydrates and fibre to help control blood sugar levels. If you don't like hot chillies, leave out the dried red ones, but keep in the green for their flavour.

5 Stir the tomatoes into the dhal and then adjust the seasoning, adding a little lemon juice to taste if necessary.

6 Add the roasted garlic purée, cumin and ground coriander, then season with salt and pepper to taste. Cook for 10–15 minutes, stirring frequently.

7 To finish the spicy garnish: melt the remaining oil in a frying pan. Add the cumin and mustard seeds and fry until the mustard seeds pop.

8 Pour the roasted seeds into the dhal, then stir in the chillies and curry leaves, swirling the mixture into the cooked dhal. Garnish with fresh coriander, and the spicy fried shallots and garlic mixture and serve hot.

Serves four

1 onion, chopped
2 green chillies, seeded and chopped
15ml/1 tbsp chopped fresh root ginger
225g/8oz/1 cup yellow or red lentils
900ml/1½ pints/3¾ cups water
45ml/3 tbsp puréed roasted garlic
5ml/1 tsp ground cumin
5ml/1 tsp ground coriander
200g/7oz tomatoes, peeled and diced
a little lemon juice
salt and ground black pepper
coriander (cilantro) sprigs, to garnish

For the spicy garnish
45ml/3 tbsp groundnut (peanut) oil
4–5 shallots, sliced
2 garlic cloves, thinly sliced
5ml/1 tsp cumin seeds
5ml/1 tsp mustard seeds
3–4 small dried red chillies
8–10 fresh curry leaves

1 First begin the spicy garnish. Heat 30ml/2 tbsp of the oil in a large, heavy pan. Add the shallots and fry them over a medium heat, stirring occasionally, until they are crisp and browned.

2 Add the garlic to the shallots and cook, stirring frequently, for a moment or two until the garlic colours slightly. Use a slotted spoon to remove the mixture from the pan and set aside.

3 To cook the dhal, add the onion, chillies and ginger to the pan and cook for 10 minutes, until golden.

4 Stir in the lentils and add the water, then bring to the boil, reduce the heat and part-cover the pan. Simmer, stirring occasionally, for 50–60 minutes, until the lentils have broken down and the dhal has a consistency similar to a very thick soup.

Energy 234kcal/979kJ; Protein 9.5g; Carbohydrate 23.8g, of which sugars 3.1g; Fat 11.8g, of which saturates 5.3g; Cholesterol 20mg; Calcium 28mg; Fibre 2.5g; Sodium 73mg.

Cabbage with bacon

You don't need much bacon, especially if it is smoked, to make all the difference to the flavour of this cabbage dish, turning it into a delicious vegetable accompaniment. Try serving it with pasta tossed with canned kidney beans for a well-balanced meal.

Serves four

30ml/2 tbsp oil
115g/4oz smoked bacon, finely chopped
1 onion, finely chopped
500g/1¼lb cabbage (red, white or Savoy)
ground black pepper

1 Heat the oil in a large pan or frying pan with a lid over a medium heat, add the bacon and cook for about 7 minutes, stirring occasionally, until crisp at the edges.

2 Add the chopped onion to the pan and cook until it becomes golden.

3 Shred the cabbage quite finely, discarding the core. Wash and drain.

4 Add the cabbage to the bacon and season with black pepper. Stir for a few minutes so that the cabbage is coated in the oil. Reduce the heat.

5 Continue to cook the cabbage, stirring frequently, for 8–10 minutes until it is tender but still crisp. If you prefer it softer, cover the pan for part of the cooking time. Serve immediately.

Cook's tips

This dish is equally delicious if you use spring greens (collards) or curly kale instead of cabbage.
  To make a substantial dish to serve for lunch or supper, add button (white) mushrooms, chunks of salad potato and skinned, seeded and chopped tomatoes.

Energy 151kcal/623kJ; Protein 6.7g; Carbohydrate 7.4g, of which sugars 7g; Fat 10.5g, of which saturates 2.6g; Cholesterol 15mg; Calcium 67mg; Fibre 2.8g; Sodium 452mg.

Cauliflower with egg and lemon

Sautéeing the cauliflower slightly before briefly cooking in water means it is full of flavour in this piquant sauce. There are so few digestible carbohydrates in cauliflower that it has no GI rating.

Serves four

30ml/2 tbsp extra virgin olive oil
1 medium cauliflower, divided into
   large florets
2 eggs
juice of 1 lemon
5ml/1 tsp cornflour (cornstarch), mixed to a
   cream with a little cold water
30ml/2 tbsp chopped fresh flat leaf parsley
salt

1 Heat the olive oil in a large heavy pan, add the cauliflower florets and sauté over a medium to high heat until they start to brown slightly.

2 Pour in enough hot water to almost cover the cauliflower, then cover the pan and cook for 7–8 minutes until the florets are just soft. Remove the pan from the heat and leave to stand, covered, while you make the sauce.

3 Beat the eggs in a bowl, add the lemon juice and cornflour and beat until mixed. Beat in a few tablespoons of the hot liquid from the cauliflower.

4 Pour the egg mixture slowly over the cauliflower, then stir gently. Place the pan over a very gentle heat for 2 minutes to thicken the sauce, but do not allow to boil. Spoon into a serving bowl, sprinkle with parsley and serve.

EAT WELL
Think of this as the new, lighter cauliflower cheese! No need to abandon the latter, but this lively dish makes a light and delicious lunch for two (not four) with chunks of wholemeal (whole-wheat) toast.
• For a delicious twist on kedgeree, poach chunks of skinless smoked haddock fillet (discard bones) with the cauliflower and serve the finished dish with basmati rice tossed with grated lemon rind and chopped fresh coriander (cilantro).

Energy 201kcal/833kJ; Protein 7g; Carbohydrate 4.4g, of which sugars 2.7g; Fat 17.5g, of which saturates 3g; Cholesterol 95mg; Calcium 51mg; Fibre 2.2g; Sodium 47mg.

Masala beans with fenugreek

The secret of this super-fast dish is the spice mixture that coats the vegetables. Cooking is kept to the minimum so that individual flavours are still detectable.

Serves four

1 onion
5ml/1 tsp ground cumin
5ml/1 tsp ground coriander
5ml/1 tsp sesame seeds
5ml/1 tsp chilli powder
2.5ml/½ tsp crushed garlic
1.5ml/¼ tsp ground turmeric
5ml/1 tsp salt
30ml/2 tbsp olive oil
1 tomato, quartered
225g/8oz/1½ cups green beans, blanched
1 bunch fresh fenugreek leaves,
   stems discarded
60ml/4 tbsp chopped fresh coriander (cilantro)
15ml/1 tbsp lemon juice

1 Roughly chop the onion. Mix together the cumin and coriander, sesame seeds, chilli powder, garlic, turmeric and salt.

2 Put the chopped onion and spice mixture into a food processor or blender, and process for 30–45 seconds until you have a rough paste.

3 In a wok or large, heavy pan, heat the oil over a medium heat and fry the spice paste for about 5 minutes, stirring the mixture occasionally.

Cook's tip
Instead of fresh fenugreek, substitute 15ml/1 tbsp dried fenugreek, and a handful of finely shredded baby spinach leaves.

4 Add the tomato quarters, blanched green beans, fresh fenugreek and chopped coriander.

5 Stir-fry the contents of the pan for about 5 minutes, then sprinkle in the lemon juice and serve.

Energy 70kcal/289kJ; Protein 1.6g; Carbohydrate 2.7g, of which sugars 2.1g; Fat 6g, of which saturates 0.7g; Cholesterol 0mg; Calcium 47mg; Fibre 2g; Sodium 6mg.

Warm bean salad with rocket

This is an easy dish, as black-eyed beans do not need to be soaked overnight. Adding spring onions and loads of dill elevates a carbohydrate and protein rich meal into something refreshing and aromatic. It can be served hot or at room temperature.

Serves four

275g/10oz/1½ cups black-eyed beans (peas)
6 spring onions (scallions), sliced
a large handful of fresh rocket (arugula) leaves, chopped if large
45–60ml/3–4 tbsp chopped fresh dill
30ml/2 tbsp extra virgin olive oil
juice of 1 lemon, or to taste
10–12 black olives
salt and ground black pepper
small cos or romaine lettuce leaves, to serve

Cook's tip
For a no-cook version, replace the black-eyed beans (peas) with canned chickpeas.

1 Thoroughly rinse the beans and drain them well. Transfer to a pan and pour in cold water to just about cover. Slowly bring to the boil over a low heat. As soon as the water is boiling, remove the pan from the heat and drain the water off immediately.

2 Put the beans back in the pan with fresh cold water to cover and add a pinch of salt – this will make their skins harder and stop them from disintegrating when they are cooked.

3 Bring the beans to the boil over a medium heat, then lower the heat and cook them until they are soft but not mushy. They will take 20–30 minutes only, so keep an eye on them.

4 Drain the beans, reserving 75–90ml/ 5–6 tbsp of the cooking liquid. Transfer the beans to a large salad bowl. Add the remaining ingredients immediately, including the reserved liquid, and mix.

5 Serve piled on the lettuce leaves, or leave to cool slightly and serve later.

Energy 238kcal/1007kJ; Protein 16.1g; Carbohydrate 31g, of which sugars 2.4g; Fat 6.4g, of which saturates 0.9g; Cholesterol 0mg; Calcium 114mg; Fibre 12.3g; Sodium 580mg.

Tomato and feta salad

This salad is a twist on a traditional Greek salad, with plenty of purslane or rocket added to the traditional combination of tomato, pepper, onion, cucumber, feta and olives. Wholemeal pitta breads are good with the salad, or serve on a bed of warm pearl barley for a main course.

Serves four

225g/8oz tomatoes

1 red onion, thinly sliced

1 green (bell) pepper, cored and sliced in thin ribbons

1 piece of cucumber, about 15cm/6in in length, peeled and sliced in rounds

150g/5oz feta cheese, cubed

a large handful of fresh purslane, trimmed of thick stalks

8–10 black olives

30ml/2 tbsp extra virgin olive oil

15ml/1 tbsp lemon juice

1.5ml/¼ tsp dried oregano

salt and ground black pepper

1 Cut the tomatoes into quarters and place them in a salad bowl. Add the onion, green pepper, cucumber, feta, purslane and olives.

2 Sprinkle the extra virgin olive oil, lemon juice and oregano on top. Add salt and ground black pepper to taste, then toss to coat everything in the olive oil and lemon, and to amalgamate the flavours of the ingredients.

3 If possible, let the salad stand for 10–15 minutes at room temperature before serving, but don't leave for too long or the cucumber will spoil.

Energy 369kcal/1528kJ; Protein 9.6g; Carbohydrate 7.7g, of which sugars 7.7g; Fat 33.5g, of which saturates 10.4g; Cholesterol 35mg; Calcium 211mg; Fibre 3g; Sodium 1303mg.

Bean salad with tuna and red onion

This classic salad makes a great main meal, with slow-release carbohydrate, protein and vitamins. For a more substantial meal, add red peppers and serve with barley, rice or bread.

Serves four

250g/9oz/1½ cups dried haricot (navy) or cannellini beans, soaked overnight in cold water
1 bay leaf
200–250g/7–9oz fine green beans, trimmed
1 large red onion, very thinly sliced
45ml/3 tbsp chopped fresh flat leaf parsley
200–250g/7–9oz good-quality canned tuna in olive oil, drained
200g/7oz cherry tomatoes, halved
salt and ground black pepper
a few onion rings, to garnish

For the dressing
45ml/3 tbsp extra virgin olive oil
15ml/1 tbsp tarragon vinegar
5ml/1 tbsp tarragon mustard
1 garlic clove, finely chopped
5ml/1 tsp grated lemon rind
a little lemon juice
pinch of caster (superfine) sugar (optional)

1 Drain the haricot or cannellini beans and bring them to the boil in a pan of fresh water with the bay leaf added. Boil rapidly for about 10 minutes, then reduce the heat and boil steadily for approximately 1–1½ hours, until tender, then drain and discard the bay leaf.

2 Place the dressing ingredients apart from the lemon juice and sugar in a jug (pitcher) or bowl and mix. Season with salt, pepper, lemon juice and a pinch of caster sugar, if you like. Leave to stand.

3 Blanch the green beans in boiling water for 3–4 minutes. Drain, refresh under cold water and drain again.

4 Place the beans in a bowl. Add half the dressing and toss. Stir in the onion and half the parsley, then season to taste. Flake the tuna and add to the beans with the tomatoes.

5 Arrange the salad on four plates. Drizzle the remaining dressing over the salad, garnish with parsley and a few onion rings and serve.

Energy 443kcal/1857kJ; Protein 29.1g; Carbohydrate 33.7g, of which sugars 6.4g; Fat 22.3g, of which saturates 3.3g; Cholesterol 25mg; Calcium 100mg; Fibre 11.9g; Sodium 162mg.

Anchovy and roasted pepper salad

Sweet peppers, salty anchovies and plenty of garlic make an intensely flavoured salad that is delicious with wholemeal pasta, rice, barley or couscous.

Serves four

2 red, 2 orange and 2 yellow (bell) peppers, halved and seeded
50g/2oz can anchovies in olive oil
2 garlic cloves
45ml/3 tbsp balsamic vinegar

Cook's tip
If you find anchovies too salty, remove them from the can, dab them dry with kitchen paper to remove most of the oil, and then place in a saucer of milk. Remove and dry again on kitchen paper once they have soaked for about 10–15 minutes, and you will find the saltiness has been reduced.

1 Preheat the oven to 200°C/400°F/ Gas 6. Place the peppers in a roasting pan and roast for 30–40 minutes. Transfer to a bowl and cover with clear film (plastic wrap).

2 When the peppers are cool, peel them and cut into strips. Drain the anchovies, reserving the oil. Halve the fillets lengthwise.

3 Slice the garlic cloves as thinly as possible and place them in a large bowl. Stir in the olive oil, balsamic vinegar and a little black pepper.

4 Add the sliced peppers and anchovy fillets and use a spoon or fork to fold the ingredients together. Cover the salad with clear film and chill until you are ready to serve.

Energy 108kcal/453kJ; Protein 6g; Carbohydrate 16.4g, of which sugars 15.5g; Fat 2.4g, of which saturates 0.5g; Cholesterol 8mg; Calcium 83mg; Fibre 4.6g; Sodium 506mg.

Main dishes

The main dishes in this chapter include satisfying and flavoursome recipes that give plenty of choice, whether you are looking for a meat-based meal, or a fish or vegetarian option. The elements of each dish are carefully balanced so that you can be sure that your fellow diners, whether diabetic or not, are getting a nutritious eating experience. There are several game recipes, as this is a lean and healthy source of protein, as well as an array of fish and vegetarian dishes. All the dishes are packed full of nutrients and flavour, providing enjoyable, healthy meals that satisfy the appetite.

Lentil and nut loaf

This might not be one of the most glamorous ways to eat lentils, but the loaf is delicious, versatile, and can be frozen after cooking, whole or cut in slices. The sharp pungency of the lemon, garlic and parsley make the perfect flavourings for the lentils and nuts.

Serves six

115g/4oz/½ cup red lentils
115g/4oz/1 cup hazelnuts
115g/4oz/1 cup walnuts
1 large carrot
2 celery sticks
1 large onion
115g/4oz/1½ cups mushrooms
45ml/3 tbsp olive oil
1 garlic clove, crushed
pinch of ground mace
30ml/2 tbsp tomato purée (paste)
grated rind of 1 lemon
1 egg, beaten
90ml/6 tbsp chopped fresh parsley
150ml/¼ pint/⅔ cup water
salt and ground black pepper
pinch of ground mace

1 Cover the lentils with cold water and soak for 1 hour. Grind the nuts in a food processor, then place them in a large bowl.

2 Coarsely chop the carrot, celery, onion and mushrooms, add to the food processor and process until all the vegetables are finely chopped.

3 Heat the olive oil in a large pan or frying pan. Add the garlic and the processed vegetable mixture and fry gently over a low heat, stirring occasionally, for 5 minutes.

4 Stir in the mace and cook for 1 minute more. Remove the pan from the heat and set aside to cool.

5 Drain the lentils and stir them into the ground nuts. Add the vegetables, tomato purée, lemon rind, egg, chopped parsley and water. Season with salt and pepper.

6 Preheat the oven to 190°C/375°F/ Gas 5. Grease a 1kg/2¼lb loaf tin (pan) and line with baking parchment or foil. Press the mixture into the tin.

7 Bake for 1–1¼ hours, until just firm, covering the top with foil if it starts to burn. Leave to stand for 15 minutes, turn out and peel off the paper.

EAT WELL
Update this traditional vegetarian favourite by serving it with a punchy vegetable salad of roasted (bell) peppers tossed with spring onions (scallions), in a dressing flavoured with mustard and dill. Serve it all on a bed of mixed leaves, and add some boiled salad potatoes for a complete meal.

Energy 422kcal/1750kJ; Protein 12.2g; Carbohydrate 19g, of which sugars 7.1g; Fat 33.6g, of which saturates 6.7g; Cholesterol 49mg; Calcium 89mg; Fibre 4.1g; Sodium 225mg.

Baked peppers with egg and Puy lentils

These oven-baked, stuffed peppers make a great main course, especially if they are served with some leafy greens. Omit the egg to make a hearty appetizer or an excellent side dish for grilled fish, pork or lamb. Red and yellow peppers have antioxidant properties and low GI rating.

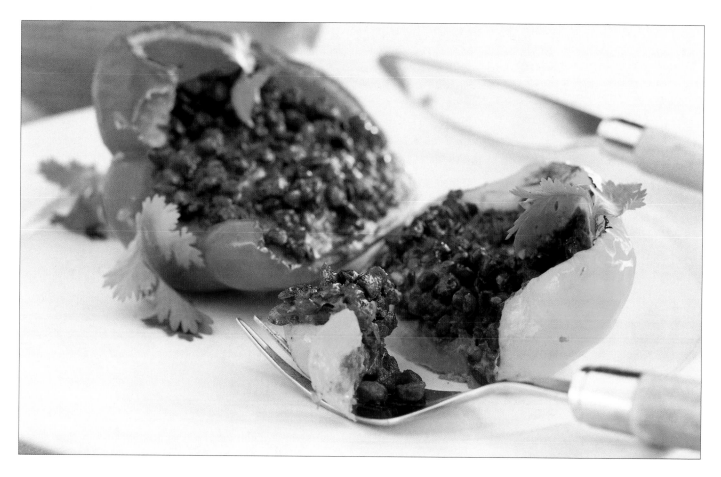

Serves four

75g/3oz/½ cup Puy lentils
2.5ml/½ tsp ground turmeric
2.5ml/½ tsp ground coriander
2.5ml/½ tsp paprika
450ml/¾ pint/1¾ cups vegetable stock
2 large (bell) peppers, halved and seeded
a little olive oil
15ml/1 tbsp chopped fresh mint
4 eggs
salt and ground black pepper
sprigs of coriander (cilantro), to garnish

EAT WELL

For a main meal, double the quantities and serve the (bell) peppers accompanied by basmati rice mixed with peas and parsley.

1 Put the Puy lentils in a large pan with the turmeric, coriander, paprika and vegetable stock.

2 Bring to the boil, stirring occasionally. Reduce the heat, part-cover the pan and simmer for 30–40 minutes. If the lentils start to dry out, add some more stock or a little water during cooking.

3 Brush the peppers lightly with a little olive oil and place them close together on a large non-stick baking tray, skin side down.

4 Preheat the oven to 190°C/375°F/ Gas 5. Stir the chopped fresh mint into the lentils, then fill the halved peppers with the lentil mixture.

5 Crack the eggs, one at a time, into a small jug (pitcher) and pour into the middle of each stuffed pepper. Stir edges of the egg white into the lentils with a fork, and sprinkle with salt and ground black pepper.

6 Bake the stuffed peppers for about 10 minutes or until the egg white is just set. Garnish with sprigs of coriander and serve immediately.

Energy 188kcal/788kJ; Protein 11.8g; Carbohydrate 16.3g, of which sugars 5.9g; Fat 9g, of which saturates 2.1g; Cholesterol 190mg; Calcium 58mg; Fibre 2.6g; Sodium 82mg.

Vegetable moussaka

This is a full-flavoured main course dish that all the family will love. It can be served with warm fresh bread and a salad and is full of ingredients to balance blood glucose levels.

Serves six

450g/1lb aubergines (eggplants), sliced
115g/4oz/½ cup whole green lentils
600ml/1 pint/2½ cups vegetable stock
1 bay leaf
45ml/3 tbsp olive oil
1 onion, sliced
1 garlic clove, crushed
225g/8oz/3¼ cups mushrooms, cleaned and
  thickly sliced
400g/14oz can chickpeas, rinsed and drained
400g/14oz can chopped tomatoes
30ml/2 tbsp tomato purée (paste)
10ml/2 tsp dried herbes de Provence
300ml/½ pint/1¼ cups natural (plain) yogurt
3 eggs
50g/2oz/½ cup grated mature Cheddar
  cheese
salt and ground black pepper
sprigs of fresh flat leaf parsley, to garnish

1 Prepare the aubergines well in advance. Cut into thin to medium slices and arrange them in a colander. You will probably find it necessary to overlap the slices or place one on top of another. Sprinkle each layer liberally with salt. Cover and place a weight or a plate on top. Leave for at least 30 minutes, to allow the bitter juices to be extracted.

EAT WELL

Mature cheeses may have more fat than some of the lightly flavoured types, but a little goes a long way, so the overall result has less fat.

2 Meanwhile, place the lentils, stock and bay leaf in a pan, cover, bring to the boil and simmer for about 20 minutes, or until the lentils are just tender but not mushy. Drain thoroughly and keep warm.

3 Heat 15ml/1 tbsp of the oil in a large pan, add the onion and garlic and cook for 5 minutes, stirring. Stir in the lentils, sliced mushrooms, chickpeas, chopped tomatoes, tomato purée, herbs and 45ml/3 tbsp water. Bring to the boil, cover and simmer gently for 10 minutes.

4 Preheat the oven to 180°C/350°F/ Gas 4. Rinse the aubergine slices, drain and pat dry. Heat the remaining oil in a frying pan and fry the slices in batches.

5 Season the lentil mixture. Layer the aubergine slices and lentil mixture alternately in a shallow ovenproof dish, starting with the aubergines. Continue the layers until all the aubergine slices and lentil mixture are used up.

6 Beat the yogurt and eggs together well, and add a little salt and plenty of ground black pepper.

7 Pour the mixture over the aubergines and lentils. Sprinkle generously with the grated Cheddar cheese and bake for about 45 minutes, or until the topping is golden brown and bubbling.

8 Serve immediately, garnished with the flat leaf parsley and accompanied by a fresh green or mixed salad, if you like.

Cook's tip

Sliced courgettes (zucchini) or potatoes can be used instead of the aubergines in this dish. Simply slice them thinly and sauté them, taking care not to break the slices.

Energy 768kcal/3255kJ; Protein 60.2g; Carbohydrate 109.6g, of which sugars 10.3g; Fat 13.1g, of which saturates 2.9g; Cholesterol 99mg; Calcium 357mg; Fibre 21.8g; Sodium 320mg.

Grilled vegetable pizza

Anyone with a gluten allergy will find all the ingredients for this pizza dough available as gluten-free versions. Home-made pizza is far healthier than bought, with generous vegetable toppings, and a thin base that provides a slow-release carbohydrate. Use low-fat cheese, if you like.

Serves six

1 courgette (zucchini), sliced
1 small aubergine (eggplant), sliced
30ml/2 tbsp olive oil
1 yellow (bell) pepper, seeded and sliced
115g/4oz/1 cup cornmeal
50g/2oz/½ cup potato flour
50g/2oz/½ cup soya flour
5ml/1 tsp baking powder
2.5ml/½ tsp salt
50g/2oz/4 tbsp butter
105ml/7 tbsp semi-skimmed (low-fat) milk
4 plum tomatoes, skinned and chopped
30ml/2 tbsp chopped fresh basil
115g/4oz mozzarella cheese, sliced
salt and ground black pepper
fresh basil sprigs, to garnish

1 Preheat the grill. Brush the courgette and aubergine slices with a little oil and place on a grill rack with the pepper slices. Cook under the grill until lightly browned, turning once.

2 Meanwhile, preheat the oven to 200°C/400°F/Gas 6. Place the cornmeal, potato flour, soya flour, baking powder and salt in a mixing bowl and stir to mix.

3 Lightly rub in the butter until the mixture resembles coarse breadcrumbs. This can also be done in the food processor. Then gradually stir in enough of the milk to make a soft, but not sticky, dough.

4 Place the dough on a sheet of baking parchment on a baking sheet and roll or press it out to form a 25cm/10in round, making the edges slightly thicker than the centre.

5 Brush the pizza dough with any remaining oil, then spread the chopped tomatoes over the dough.

6 Sprinkle the chopped plum tomato with the chopped basil and season with salt and pepper. Arrange the grilled vegetables over the herbs and top with the cheese.

7 Bake for 25–30 minutes until crisp and golden brown. Garnish the pizza with fresh basil sprigs and serve immediately, cut into slices.

Cook's tip
Instead of cornmeal, potato and soya flours, use 225g/8oz/2 cups of half plain (all-purpose) and half wholemeal (whole-wheat) flours.

Energy 400kcal/1666kJ; Protein 11.9g; Carbohydrate 34.6g, of which sugars 9.6g; Fat 23.9g, of which saturates 5.3g; Cholesterol 18mg; Calcium 166mg; Fibre 4.4g; Sodium 240mg.

Mediterranean one-crust pie

This free-form crust is the easiest way to make a pie. It encases a rich and hearty tomato, aubergine and kidney bean filling in a wholemeal cheese pastry.

Serves four

500g/1¼lb aubergine (eggplant), cubed
1 red (bell) pepper
30ml/2 tbsp olive oil
1 large onion, finely chopped
1 courgette (zucchini), sliced
2 garlic cloves, crushed
15ml/1 tbsp fresh oregano or 5ml/1 tsp
  dried, plus fresh oregano leaves to garnish
200g/7oz/1½ cups canned red kidney beans,
  drained and rinsed
115g/4oz/1 cup pitted black olives, rinsed
375g/13oz/⅔ cup passata (bottled, strained
  tomatoes)
1 egg, beaten, or a little milk
30ml/2 tbsp semolina
salt and ground black pepper

For the pastry
75g/3oz/⅔ cup plain (all-purpose) flour
75g/3oz/⅔ cup wholemeal (whole-wheat)
  flour
75g/3oz/6 tbsp butter
25g/1oz/⅓ cup grated Parmesan cheese

5 Heat the oil in a large heavy frying pan. Fry the onions for 5 minutes until softened. Add the aubergine and fry for 5 minutes. Add the courgettes, garlic and oregano, and cook for a further 5 minutes, stirring frequently. Add the beans and olives, stir, then add the passata and pepper. Cook until heated through, and set aside to cool.

1 Preheat the oven to 220°C/425°F/ Gas 7. To make the pastry, sift the plain and wholemeal flours into a large bowl. Rub in the butter until the mixture resembles fine breadcrumbs, then stir in the grated Parmesan. Mix in enough cold water to form a firm dough.

2 Turn out the dough on to a lightly floured work surface and form into a smooth ball. Wrap the dough in clear film (plastic wrap) or a plastic bag and chill for about 30 minutes.

3 To make the filling, place the aubergine in a colander and sprinkle with salt, then leave for about 30 minutes. Rinse them, drain, and pat dry with kitchen paper.

4 Meanwhile, place the pepper on a baking tray and roast in the oven for 20 minutes, until the skin is slightly charred and the flesh is soft. Put the pepper in a plastic bag and leave until cool enough to handle. Peel and seed, then dice the flesh. Set aside.

6 Roll out the pastry on a lightly floured board to form a rough 30cm/12in round. Place on a lightly oiled baking sheet. Brush with beaten egg, sprinkle on the semolina, leaving a 4cm/1½in border, then spoon in the filling.

7 Gather up the edges of the pastry to partly cover the filling – it should be open in the middle. Brush with the remaining egg or milk and bake for 30–35 minutes until golden. Garnish with oregano.

Energy 554kcal/2318kJ; Protein 17.7g; Carbohydrate 56.6g, of which sugars 15.7g; Fat 30.2g, of which saturates 4.2g; Cholesterol 13mg; Calcium 295mg; Fibre 11.6g; Sodium 1353mg.

Roast monkfish with garlic

The combination of monkfish and garlic is superb and makes a good low-fat alternative to a traditional meat-based meal. Serve with vibrant greens or canned flageolet beans.

Serves four

1kg/2¼ lb monkfish tail, skinned
14 fat garlic cloves
5ml/1 tsp fresh thyme leaves
30ml/2 tbsp olive oil
juice of 1 lemon
2 bay leaves
salt and ground black pepper

1 Preheat the oven to 220°C/425°F/ Gas 7. Remove any membrane from the fish and cut out the central bone.

2 Peel two garlic cloves and cut them into thin slivers. Scatter a quarter of the garlic slices and half of the thyme leaves over the cut side of the fish, then close it up and use fine kitchen string to tie it into a neat shape, like a boned, rolled piece of meat. Pat the fish dry with kitchen paper.

3 Make incisions on either side of the fish and push in the remaining garlic slivers. Heat half the olive oil in a frying pan which can safely be transferred to the oven. When the oil is very hot, put the monkfish into the pan and brown it all over for about 5 minutes, until it is evenly coloured.

4 Season the fish with salt and pepper, sprinkle with lemon juice and scatter over the remaining thyme.

5 Tuck the bay leaves under the monkfish, arrange the unpeeled garlic cloves around it and drizzle the remaining olive oil over. Transfer the frying pan to the oven and roast for 20–25 minutes, until cooked through.

6 Place on a warmed serving dish with the garlic and some green beans. To serve, remove the string and cut the monkfish into thick slices.

EAT WELL

For a special occasion, par-boil small new potatoes until half cooked, then drain and toss with 1–2 tbsp olive oil on a roasting pan. Roast in the oven until crisp and well browned. They are good as an alternative to chips (French fries).

Energy 173kcal/727kJ; Protein 30.5g; Carbohydrate 2.7g, of which sugars 0.3g; Fat 4.4g, of which saturates 0.7g; Cholesterol 27mg; Calcium 18mg; Fibre 0.7g; Sodium 34mg.

Cod with pancetta and butter beans

Cod steaks wrapped in pancetta and roasted are superb accompanied by butter beans and tomatoes – a combination of low GI carbohydrates and low-fat protein for a balanced meal.

Serves four

200g/7oz/1 cup dried butter (lima) beans,
    soaked overnight in cold water to cover
2 leeks, thinly sliced
2 garlic cloves, chopped
8 fresh sage leaves
45ml/3 tbsp fruity olive oil
8 thin slices of pancetta
4 thick cod steaks, skinned
12 cherry tomatoes
salt and ground black pepper

1 Drain the beans, tip into a pan and cover with cold water. Bring to the boil and skim off the foam on the surface. Lower the heat, then stir in the leeks, garlic and four sage leaves. Simmer for 1–1½ hours until the beans are tender, adding more water if necessary. Drain, return to the pan, season, stir in 15ml/ 1 tbsp olive oil and keep warm.

2 Preheat the oven to 200ºC/400ºF/ Gas 6. Wrap two slices of pancetta around the edge of each cod steak, tying it on with kitchen string or securing it with a wooden cocktail stick (toothpick). Insert a sage leaf between the pancetta and the cod. Season the fish with salt and pepper.

Cook's tips
Use cannellini beans in place of butter (lima) beans, and streaky bacon instead of pancetta. Use haddock or salmon instead of cod.

3 Heat a heavy frying pan, add 15ml/ 1 tbsp of the remaining oil and seal the cod steaks two at a time for 1 minute on each side. Transfer the steaks to an ovenproof dish and roast in the oven for 5 minutes.

4 Add the tomatoes to the dish and drizzle over the remaining olive oil. Roast for 5 minutes more, until the cod steaks are cooked but still juicy. Serve them on a bed of butter beans with the roasted tomatoes. Garnish with parsley.

EAT WELL
To add valuable vegetable content to this dish, serve it with a big pile of freshly cooked green beans tossed with lemon juice and topped with chopped chives and black pepper.

Energy 449kcal/1883kJ; Protein 44.5g; Carbohydrate 25.3g, of which sugars 3.9g; Fat 19.5g, of which saturates 3g; Cholesterol 84mg; Calcium 85mg; Fibre 9.8g; Sodium 403mg.

Filo fish pies

Filo makes a good alternative to puff pastry, or even shortcrust, and it makes a fabulous case for light-textured fish. Serve with roasted sweet potatoes for some slow-release carbohydrate.

Serves six

400g/14oz spinach, trimmed
1 egg, lightly beaten
2 garlic cloves, crushed
450g/1lb white fish fillet
juice of 1 lemon
olive oil
8–12 filo pastry sheets, thawed if frozen,
   quartered
15ml/1 tbsp finely chopped fresh chives
200ml/7fl oz/scant 1 cup half-fat
   crème fraîche
15ml/1 tbsp chopped fresh dill
salt and ground black pepper

Tips and twists

If you prefer to make one large pie, use a 20cm/8in tin (pan) and bake for around 45 minutes.

1 Preheat the oven to 190°C/375°F/ Gas 5. Wash the spinach, then cook in a lidded pan with just the water that clings to the leaves. When wilted, drain, squeeze as dry as possible and chop.

2 Put the spinach in a bowl, add the egg and garlic, season with salt and pepper and set aside. Cut the fish into small pieces and place in a bowl. Stir in the lemon juice. Season with salt and pepper and toss lightly.

3 Brush the inside of six 13cm/5in tartlet tins (muffin pans) with a little olive oil. Fit a piece of filo pastry into the tins, draping it so it hangs over the sides. Brush with a little olive oil, then add another sheet at right angles to the first. Continue to line the tins in this way.

4 Spread the spinach evenly over the pastry. Add the diced fish and season well. Stir the chives into the crème fraîche and spread the mixture over the top of the fish. Scatter the dill over.

5 Draw the overhanging pieces of pastry together and scrunch lightly to make a lid. Brush sparsely with oil. Bake for about 15–20 minutes, until golden brown.

Energy 233kcal/972kJ; Protein 18.4g; Carbohydrate 9.1g, of which sugars 2.2g; Fat 14g, of which saturates 8.2g; Cholesterol 84mg; Calcium 170mg; Fibre 1.7g; Sodium 213mg.

Warm swordfish and rocket salad

Swordfish is robust enough to take the sharp flavours of rocket and Pecorino cheese. If you can't find Pecorino, use a good Parmesan, both of which are relatively low fat cheeses.

Serves four

4 swordfish steaks, about 175g/6oz each
75ml/5 tbsp extra virgin olive oil, plus extra
    for serving
juice of 1 lemon
30ml/2 tbsp finely chopped fresh parsley
115g/4oz rocket (arugula) leaves
115g/4oz Pecorino cheese
salt and ground black pepper

1 Lay the swordfish in a shallow dish. Mix 60ml/4 tbsp of the olive oil with the lemon juice. Pour over the fish. Season, sprinkle on the parsley and turn the fish to coat, cover with clear film (plastic wrap) and marinate for 10 minutes.

2 Heat a griddle until very hot. Take the fish out of the marinade and pat it dry with kitchen paper. Grill for 2–3 minutes on each side until the swordfish is just cooked through, but still juicy.

Cook's tip
Tuna or shark steaks would be equally good in this recipe.

3 Meanwhile, put the rocket leaves in a bowl and season with a little salt and plenty of pepper. Add the remaining 15ml/1 tbsp olive oil and toss well. Shave the Pecorino over the top of the tossed rocket salad.

4 Place the swordfish steaks on four individual plates and arrange a little pile of salad on each steak.

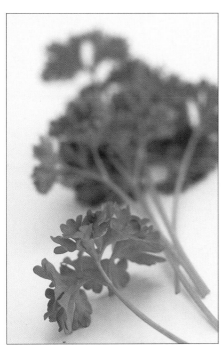

Energy 452kcal/1880kJ; Protein 43.6g; Carbohydrate 0.5g, of which sugars 0.4g; Fat 30.6g, of which saturates 9.5g; Cholesterol 101mg; Calcium 401mg; Fibre 0.6g; Sodium 581mg.

Fish pie

This fish pie can be varied to suit your eating preferences: for example, use olive oil in the mashed potatoes for a delicious, healthy alternative to butter, and omit the cheese.

Serves four

450g/1lb cod or haddock fillets
225g/8oz smoked cod fillets
300ml/½ pint/1¼ cups milk
½ lemon, sliced
1 bay leaf
1 fresh thyme sprig
4–5 black peppercorns
50g/2oz/¼ cup butter
25g/1oz/¼ cup plain (all-purpose) flour
30ml/2 tbsp chopped fresh parsley
5ml/1 tsp anchovy essence
150g/5oz/2 cups shiitake or brown cap
  (cremini) mushrooms, sliced
salt, ground black pepper and cayenne pepper

For the topping
450g/1lb potatoes, cooked and mashed
  with milk
30ml/2 tbsp olive oil
2 tomatoes, sliced
25g/1oz/¼ cup grated Cheddar cheese
  (optional)

1 Put the fish skin side down in a shallow pan. Add the milk, lemon slices, bay leaf, thyme and peppercorns.

2 Bring to the boil, then lower the heat and poach gently for about 5 minutes, until just cooked. Strain off and reserve the milk. Remove the fish skin and flake the flesh, discarding any bones.

3 Melt half the butter in a small pan, stir in the flour and cook gently for 1 minute. Add the milk and boil, whisking, until smooth and creamy.

4 Stir the parsley and anchovy essence into the sauce, season to taste.

5 Heat the remaining butter in a frying pan, add the sliced mushrooms and sauté until tender. Season and add to the flaked fish. Mix the sauce into the fish and stir gently to combine. Transfer the mixture to an ovenproof casserole.

6 Preheat the oven to 200°C/400°F/ Gas 6. Beat the mashed potato with the olive oil until very creamy. Season, then spread the topping evenly over the fish. Fork up the surface and arrange the sliced tomatoes around the edge. Sprinkle with grated cheese, if using.

7 Bake for 20–25 minutes, until the topping is browned. If you prefer, finish the browning under a hot grill (broiler).

EAT WELL
Add finely chopped barely cooked broccoli and spring onions (scallions) to mashed potato for a healthy, full-flavoured pie top.

Energy 458kcal/1921kJ; Protein 29.5g; Carbohydrate 32.8g, of which sugars 5.8g; Fat 25g, of which saturates 3.7g; Cholesterol 74mg; Calcium 216mg; Fibre 1g; Sodium 867mg.

Cod caramba

This colourful Mexican dish, with its contrasting crunchy topping and tender fish filling, provides lots of vegetable food value, and is good accompanied by rice and red kidney beans.

Serves four

450g/1lb cod fillets
225g/8oz smoked cod fillets
300ml/½ pint/1¼ cups fish stock
30ml/2 tbsp olive oil
1 onion, sliced
2 garlic cloves, crushed
1 green and 1 red (bell) pepper, diced
2 courgettes (zucchini), diced
115g/4oz/⅔ cup drained canned or thawed
    frozen corn kernels
2 tomatoes, peeled and chopped
juice of 1 lime
Tabasco sauce
salt, ground black pepper and
    cayenne pepper

For the topping
75g/3oz tortilla chips
50g/2oz/½ cup grated Cheddar cheese
coriander (cilantro) sprigs, to garnish
lime wedges, to serve

1 Lay the fish in a shallow pan and pour over the fish stock. Bring to the boil, lower the heat, cover and poach for about 8 minutes, until the flesh flakes easily when tested with the tip of a sharp knife. Leave to cool slightly, then remove the skin and separate the flesh into large flakes. Keep hot.

2 Heat the olive oil in a pan, add the onion and garlic and cook over a low heat until soft. Add the peppers, stir and cook for 2 minutes. Stir in the courgettes and cook for 3 minutes more, until all the vegetables are tender.

3 Stir in the corn and tomatoes, then add lime juice and Tabasco to taste. Season with a little salt, black pepper and cayenne.

4 Cook for a couple of minutes to heat the corn and tomatoes, then stir in the fish and transfer to a dish that can safely be used under the grill (broiler).

5 Preheat the grill. Make the topping by crushing the tortilla chips, then mixing in the grated cheese. Add cayenne pepper and sprinkle over the fish.

6 Place the dish under the grill until the topping is crisp and brown. Serve, garnished with coriander sprigs and lime wedges.

Energy 293kcal/1223kJ; Protein 26.6g; Carbohydrate 15.8g, of which sugars 7.5g; Fat 13.9g, of which saturates 6.9g; Cholesterol 78mg; Calcium 123mg; Fibre 3.2g; Sodium 927mg.

Black bean chilli con carne

Fresh green and dried red chillies add plenty of fire to this classic Tex-Mex dish of tender beef cooked in a spicy tomato sauce. Serve with rice or baked potatoes for a low GI meal.

Serves six

225g/8oz/1¼ cups dried black beans
500g/1¼lb braising steak
30ml/2 tbsp vegetable oil
2 onions, chopped
1 garlic clove, crushed
1 fresh green chilli, seeded and
   finely chopped
15ml/1 tbsp paprika
10ml/2 tsp ground cumin
10ml/2 tsp ground coriander
400g/14oz can chopped tomatoes
300ml/½ pint/1¼ cups beef stock
1 dried red chilli, crumbled
5ml/1 tsp hot pepper sauce
1 fresh red (bell) pepper, seeded and chopped
salt
fresh coriander (cilantro), to garnish
boiled rice, to serve

1 Put the beans in a large pan. Add enough cold water to cover them, bring to the boil and boil vigorously for about 10 minutes. Drain, transfer to a clean bowl, cover with cold water and leave to soak for about 8 hours or overnight.

2 Preheat the oven to 150°C/300°F/ Gas 2. Cut the braising steak into small dice. Heat the vegetable oil in a large, flameproof casserole. Add the chopped onion, crushed garlic and chopped green chilli and cook them gently for 5 minutes until soft, using a slotted spoon to transfer the mixture to a plate.

3 Increase the heat to high, add the meat to the casserole and brown on all sides, then stir in the paprika, ground cumin and ground coriander.

4 Add the tomatoes, beef stock, dried chilli and hot pepper sauce. Drain the beans and add them to the casserole, with enough water to cover.

5 Bring the casserole to simmering point, cover and cook in the oven for 2 hours. Stir occasionally and add extra water, if necessary.

6 Season the casserole with salt and add the chopped red pepper. Replace the lid, return the casserole to the oven and cook for 30 minutes more, or until the meat and beans are tender. Sprinkle over the fresh coriander and serve with rice.

EAT WELL
This is also good made with chopped chicken or turkey breast fillet, without skin, for a low-fat main course.

Cook's tips
Red kidney beans are traditionally used in chilli con carne, but in this recipe black beans are used instead. They are the same shape and size as red kidney beans but have a shiny black skin. They are also known as Mexican or Spanish black beans.
  Use minced (ground) beef in place of the braising steak.

Energy 289kcal/1216kJ; Protein 27.3g; Carbohydrate 24.7g, of which sugars 7.9g; Fat 9.7g, of which saturates 2.8g; Cholesterol 45mg; Calcium 61mg; Fibre 7.8g; Sodium 65mg.

Fried rice with beef

A little meat goes a long way in stir-fry dishes. Tossed with rice and broccoli, this dish has enough beef for flavour and it also helps to slow down the rate at which the rice is digested.

Serves four

200g/7oz lean beef steak, chilled
15ml/1 tbsp vegetable oil
2 garlic cloves, finely chopped
1 egg
250g/9oz/2¼ cups cooked jasmine rice
2 heads broccoli, coarsely chopped
30ml/2 tbsp dark soy sauce
15ml/1 tbsp light soy sauce
15ml/1 tbsp Thai fish sauce
ground black pepper
chilli sauce, to serve

1 Trim the steak and cut it, across the grain of the meat, into very thin strips with a sharp knife.

2 Heat the oil in a wok or frying pan and cook the garlic over a low to medium heat until golden. Do not let it burn. Increase the heat to high, add the steak and stir-fry for 2 minutes.

3 Move the pieces of beef to the edges of the wok or pan and break the egg into the centre. When the egg starts to set, stir-fry it with the meat.

4 Add the rice and toss all the contents of the wok together, scraping up any residue on the base, then add the broccoli, soy sauces, sugar and fish sauce and stir-fry for 2 minutes more.

5 Season to taste with pepper and serve immediately with chilli sauce.

EAT WELL
Be generous with vegetables and mean with meat in stir-fries. Add crisp mangetouts (snow peas) or sticks of carrot and red (bell) pepper for a good mix of nutrients.

Cook's tip
Soy sauce is made from fermented soya beans. The first extraction is sold as light soy sauce and has a delicate fragrance. Dark soy has been allowed to mature for longer.

Energy 385kcal/1606kJ; Protein 20.7g; Carbohydrate 52.7g, of which sugars 2.5g; Fat 9.8g, of which saturates 2.8g; Cholesterol 81mg; Calcium 59mg; Fibre 1.6g; Sodium 590mg.

Chunky burgers with spicy relish

These home-made burgers are a much healthier alternative to high-fat commercial types. Wholemeal breadcrumbs add bulk to the lean beef, and serving with tomato relish adds vitamins.

Serves four

350g/12oz lean minced (ground) beef
1 onion, chopped
30ml/2 tbsp chopped fresh flat leaf parsley
30ml/2 tbsp tomato purée (paste)
100g/4oz fresh wholemeal (whole-wheat) breadcrumbs
1 egg, beaten
salt and ground black pepper
4 burger buns
1 Little Gem (Bibb) lettuce, separated

For the spicy relish
15ml/1 tbsp olive oil
1 shallot, chopped
1 garlic clove, crushed
1 small green chilli, seeded and finely chopped
8 very ripe tomatoes, skinned and chopped

1 In a large bowl, place the minced beef, onion, parsley, tomato purée, breadcrumbs, egg and seasoning, then use your hands to mix until it is thoroughly combined.

2 Divide the mixture into quarters and shape into chunky burgers, pressing them firmly between your hands.

3 To make the relish, heat the olive oil in a pan and cook the shallot, garlic and chilli for a few minutes, stirring, until softened. Stir in the chopped fresh tomatoes and simmer for 10 minutes.

4 Meanwhile, preheat the grill (broiler), a griddle or frying pan. Grill (broil) or fry the burgers for about 5 minutes on each side, or until cooked through. Keep warm.

5 Split and lightly toast the buns on the inside. Arrange a few lettuce leaves on the bases, then top with the burgers. Add a dollop of warm spicy relish. Replace the bun tops and serve, offering the remaining relish and extra lettuce leaves separately.

Italian meatballs

Oats help bulk out the meat, and add some slow-release carbohydrate. Serve with a good portion of red peppers and a generous serving of pasta for a healthy balance.

Serves four

10ml/2 tsp sunflower oil
1 large onion, chopped
2 garlic cloves, finely chopped
15ml/1 tbsp fresh thyme leaves
450g/1lb lean minced (ground) beef
100g/4oz rolled oats
1 large egg
salt and ground black pepper
fresh thyme leaves, to garnish

For the sauce
4 red (bell) peppers, halved and seeded
1 onion, quartered
400g/14oz can chopped tomatoes

1 Heat the oil in a frying pan and cook the onion and garlic for 5 minutes, or until softened. Remove the pan from the heat and add the thyme, then turn the mixture into a bowl.

2 Add the minced beef, rolled oats, egg and seasoning to the onion mixture. Mix until all the ingredients are thoroughly combined.

3 Use your hands to shape the mixture into 20 small meatballs, then chill them until the sauce is ready.

4 To make the sauce, preheat the grill (broiler). Arrange the peppers on a rack with the pieces of onion. Grill (broil) for 12–15 minutes, turning frequently, or until the pepper skins are blackened.

5 Remove the grill from the heat, cover the peppers with a dish towel and leave to cool. Peel the peppers and place them in a blender or food processor with the grilled onion and the tomatoes. Process until smooth, then add seasoning to taste.

6 Cook the meatballs in a large, non-stick frying pan for about 10–15 minutes, gently rolling them around to brown them evenly all over.

7 Add the puréed pepper and tomato mixture and bring to the boil, then reduce the heat and simmer for 10 minutes, turning the balls to coat once or twice during cooking. Transfer to a dish and scatter with thyme leaves to garnish, then serve at once.

Energy 484kcal/2021kJ; Protein 27.9g; Carbohydrate 30.2g, of which sugars 7.7g; Fat 28.8g, of which saturates 9.3g; Cholesterol 68mg; Calcium 120mg; Fibre 2.2g; Sodium 473mg.
Energy 341kcal/1427kJ; Protein 33g; Carbohydrate 18.3g, of which sugars 12.9g; Fat 15.5g, of which saturates 5.6g; Cholesterol 120mg; Calcium 44mg; Fibre 3.7g; Sodium 160mg.

Beef casserole

Adding a good amount of mushrooms to this dish bulks out a modest portion of meat, keeping the dish full flavoured and balancing protein and vegetables. The traditional accompaniment is creamy mashed potate, but a healthier choice would be leafy greens and brown rice.

Serves four

450g/1lb lean stewing beef
25g/1oz/¼ cup plain (all-purpose) flour
2.5ml/½ tsp paprika
45ml/3 tbsp sunflower oil
2 large onions, peeled and chopped
350g/12oz button (white) mushrooms, quartered
2 garlic cloves, crushed with a little salt
grated rind of 1 orange
300ml/½ pint/1¼ cups red wine
150ml/¼ pint/⅔ cup beef stock
salt and ground black pepper

1 Preheat the oven to 180ºC/350ºF/ Gas 4. Cut the meat into cubes.

2 Mix the flour with salt, pepper and paprika, spread on a tray or large plate, and coat the meat.

3 Heat a large pan, add 30ml/2 tbsp of the oil and brown the meat. Do this in batches if your pan is small.

4 Transfer the meat to a casserole. Brown the onions in the fat in the pan. Add the onions to the casserole. Keeping the pan hot, add the rest of the oil and brown the mushrooms. Add to the casserole.

5 Add the rest of the ingredients to the casserole and bring to the boil, stirring to combine the orange rind and evenly distribute the meat and mushrooms.

6 Cover the casserole and place in the preheated oven for about 3 hours, until the meat is tender. Serve with mashed potato or brown rice and lots of steamed leafy green vegetables.

Energy 457kcal/1905kJ; Protein 36.8g; Carbohydrate 12.2g, of which sugars 4.7g; Fat 20g, of which saturates 6.5g; Cholesterol 87mg; Calcium 78mg; Fibre 2.3g; Sodium 169mg.

Roast lamb with beans

Roasting the lamb slowly on a bed of beans results in a dish that combines meltingly tender meat with low GI carbohydrate all in one pot. Serve with seasonal vegetables.

Serves six

8–10 garlic cloves, peeled
1.8–2kg/4–4½lb leg of lamb
30ml/2 tbsp olive oil
450g/1lb spinach leaves
2 x 400g/14oz cans flageolet, cannellini or
  haricot (navy) beans, drained
400g/14oz can butter (lima) beans, drained
2 large, fresh rosemary sprigs, plus extra
  to garnish
15–30ml/1–2 tbsp drained, bottled
  green peppercorns

1 Preheat the oven to 150°C/300°F/ Gas 2. Set four garlic cloves aside and slice the rest lengthways into three or four pieces. Make shallow slits in the skin of the lamb and insert a piece of garlic into each.

2 Heat the olive oil in a heavy, shallow flameproof casserole or a roasting pan that is large enough to hold the leg of lamb. Add the reserved garlic cloves and the fresh spinach leaves to the casserole or pan.

3 Cook over a medium heat, stirring occasionally, for 4–5 minutes, or until the spinach is wilted.

4 Add the beans and tuck the rosemary sprigs and peppercorns among them. Place the lamb on top, then cover the casserole or pan with foil or a lid.

5 Roast the lamb for 3–4 hours until it is cooked to your taste. Slice the lamb and serve it hot with the beans, garnished with the remaining fresh rosemary sprigs.

Energy 705kcal/2945kJ; Protein 74.3g; Carbohydrate 22.2g, of which sugars 4.2g; Fat 35.9g, of which saturates 15.4g; Cholesterol 246mg; Calcium 186mg; Fibre 8.7g; Sodium 775mg.

Pork tenderloin with Puy lentils

Pork has become one of the leanest meats and the tenderloin is free from visible fat. Puy lentils are a good source of low GI carbohydrate and delicious in this spicy sauce.

Serves four

500g/1¼lb pork tenderloin
15ml/1 tbsp sunflower oil
8–12 large spinach leaves
1 onion, chopped
1 garlic clove, finely chopped
2.5cm/1in piece fresh root ginger, finely grated
1 red chilli, finely chopped (optional)
250g/9oz/generous 1 cup Puy lentils
750ml/1¼ pints/3 cups chicken or vegetable stock
200ml/7fl oz/scant 1 cup milk
salt and ground black pepper

1 Cut the pork tenderloin widthways into two equal pieces. Season the pork well with salt and ground black pepper.

EAT WELL
Serve the pork with a stir-fry of red onion, red (bell) peppers, beetroot (beet) (cooked and cut into sticks), shredded red cabbage and carrots. The protein and lentils help to slow down the digestion of the carbohydrate from high GI ingredients such as carrots.

Cook's tip
Wrap the pork in slices of prosciutto, instead of the spinach leaves, and secure with wooden cocktail sticks (toothpicks).

2 Preheat the oven to 180°C/350°F/ Gas 4. Heat the oil in a frying pan, add the pork and brown over a high heat on all sides. Remove the meat from the pan and set aside.

3 Meanwhile, place the spinach leaves one by one, so they stay separate, into a large pan of boiling water and cook for 1 minute, or until just wilted. Drain immediately in a colander and refresh under cold running water. Drain well.

4 Lay the cooked, cooled spinach leaves on the work surface, overlapping them slightly to form a rectangle. Place the pork tenderloin on top and wrap the leaves around the pork to enclose it completely.

5 Add the onion to the oil in the frying pan and cook for about 5 minutes, stirring occasionally, until softened. Add the chopped garlic, grated ginger and finely chopped chilli, if using, and fry for a further 1 minute.

6 Add the lentils to the onion mixture in the frying pan and then stir in the chicken or vegetable stock. Bring to the boil, then boil rapidly for 10 minutes. Remove the pan from the heat and stir in the milk. Transfer the onion and lentil mixture to a casserole and arrange the pork tenderloins on top.

7 Cover the casserole and place it in the oven. Cook for 45 minutes, or until the lentils are cooked.

8 To serve, remove the spinach-wrapped pork tenderloins from the casserole using a slotted spoon or tongs and cut the pork into thick slices.

9 Stir the lentils and spoon them, with some of the cooking juices, on to warmed, individual plates and top each portion with a few of the pork slices.

Energy 399kcal/1683kJ; Protein 42.3g; Carbohydrate 39.1g, of which sugars 5g; Fat 9.2g, of which saturates 4g; Cholesterol 87mg; Calcium 81mg; Fibre 3.5g; Sodium 206mg.

Baked ham with parsley sauce

A whole joint of ham is delicious boiled with buttered cabbage and a classic parsley sauce. Serve modest portions of meat with lots of vegetables and use any left-over slices in sandwiches with lots of salad, or diced to flavour a mixed vegetable stir-fry.

Serves six

1.3kg/3lb bacon or gammon
1 carrot, chopped
2 celery sticks, chopped
2 leeks, chopped
5ml/1 tsp peppercorns
15ml/1 tbsp oven-dried breadcrumbs
15ml/1 tbsp English mustard
7.5ml/1½ tsp light muscovado (brown) sugar
25g/1oz/2 tbsp butter
900g/2lb green cabbage, sliced

For the parsley sauce
25g/1oz/2 tbsp butter
25g/1oz/¼ cup plain (all-purpose) flour
300ml/½ pint/1¼ cups half cooking liquid and half milk
bunch of parsley, leaves chopped
ground black pepper

1 Place the bacon joint in a large pan. Add the vegetables to the pan, with the peppercorns. Cover with cold water and bring to the boil. Simmer gently for about 20 minutes per 450g/1lb. Preheat the oven to 200°C/400°F/Gas 6.

EAT WELL
Boiled new potatoes and mashed carrot and swede (rutabaga) are great with bacon or ham. Instead of using butter when mashing, add plenty of black pepper and drizzle in a little olive oil. Served with meat, the high GI value of carrots and swede is balanced and they may not swing blood glucose as drastically as they can do.

2 Remove the joint from the pan, reserving the cooking liquid. Cut off the rind, and score the fat. Place in a roasting pan. Mix the breadcrumbs, mustard, sugar and 15g/½oz/1 tbsp butter; spread over the joint. Place in the oven for 15–20 minutes.

3 To make the parsley sauce, melt the butter in a pan, add the flour and cook for 1–2 minutes, stirring constantly. Gradually whisk in the cooking liquid and milk. Bring to the boil and simmer for 3–4 minutes, then stir in the parsley. Season to taste with pepper.

4 In a large pan cook the cabbage with a little of the cooking liquid from the bacon. Drain well, season to taste and toss in the remaining butter.

5 To serve, slice the bacon and serve on a bed of cabbage, with a little of the parsley sauce.

Energy 689kcal/2857kJ; Protein 40.4g; Carbohydrate 16.3g, of which sugars 10.6g; Fat 51.5g, of which saturates 23.1g; Cholesterol 155mg; Calcium 139mg; Fibre 5g; Sodium 3461mg.

Ostrich casserole with chickpeas

Lean and firm, ostrich meat is full-flavoured and delicious with the soft-textured sweet potatoes and chickpeas in this quick and easy, satisfying low-GI stew. If you cannot find ostrich meat, substitute any lean red meat, such as venison or beef.

Serves four

45ml/3 tbsp olive oil
1 large onion, chopped
2 garlic cloves, finely chopped
450g/1lb ostrich fillet, cut into short strips
450g/1lb sweet potatoes, peeled and diced
2 x 400g/14oz cans chopped tomatoes
400g/14oz can chickpeas, drained
salt and ground black pepper
fresh oregano, to garnish

Eat well

Couscous is a quick and easy carbohydrate accompaniment. For a rounded meal, serve a good mixed fruit salad to follow.

1 Heat half the oil in a flameproof casserole. Add the chopped onion and garlic, and cook for about 5 minutes until softened but not coloured.

2 Remove the onions and garlic from the casserole using a slotted spoon and set aside. Add the remaining oil to the casserole and heat.

3 Brown the meat in batches over a high heat. When the last batch is cooked, replace all the meat and the onions in the casserole, with the potatoes, tomatoes and chickpeas.

4 Bring to the boil, reduce the heat and simmer for 25 minutes. Season and serve garnished with the fresh oregano.

Energy 639kcal/2682kJ; Protein 49g; Carbohydrate 51.2g, of which sugars 16.5g; Fat 27.9g, of which saturates 8.2g; Cholesterol 98mg; Calcium 108mg; Fibre 9.7g; Sodium 393mg.

Roast chicken and vegetables

This is a delicious, vegetable-rich alternative to traditional roast chicken. The recipe also works
very well with guinea fowl. Root vegetables can also be used instead of Mediterranean varieties.

4 Arrange the potatoes around the
chicken and roll them in the cooking
juices until they are thoroughly coated.
Return the pan to the hot oven to
continue roasting.

5 After 30 minutes, add the aubergine,
red pepper, fennel and garlic cloves to
the pan. Drizzle the vegetables with the
remaining oil, and season to taste with
salt and pepper.

6 Add the remaining sprigs of thyme
to the pan, tucking the sprigs in among
the vegetables. Return the chicken and
vegetables to the oven and cook for
30–50 minutes more, basting and
turning the vegetables occasionally
during cooking.

Serves four

1.8–2.25kg/4–5lb roasting chicken
30ml/2 tbsp extra virgin olive oil
½ lemon
a few sprigs of fresh thyme
675g/1½lb small new potatoes
1 aubergine (eggplant), cut into 2.5cm/
   1in cubes
2 red or yellow (bell) peppers, seeded
   and quartered
2 fennel bulbs, trimmed and quartered
8 large garlic cloves, unpeeled
coarse salt and ground black pepper

1 Preheat the oven to 200°C/400°F/
Gas 6. Rub the chicken all over with
olive oil and season with pepper. Place
the lemon half inside the bird, with a
sprig or two of thyme.

2 Put the chicken breast side down in a
large roasting pan. Place in the oven
and roast for about 30 minutes.

3 Remove the chicken from the oven
and season with salt. Turn the chicken
right side up, and baste with the juices
from the pan.

7 To find out if the chicken is cooked,
push the tip of a small sharp knife
between the thigh and breast – if the
juices run clear, rather than pink, it is
done. The vegetables should be tender
and beginning to brown. Let the
chicken stand for 20 minutes, keeping
the vegetables warm, before carving.
Serve with a green vegetable.

Energy 798kcal/3310kJ; Protein 43.3g; Carbohydrate 23.7g, of which sugars 6.1g; Fat 59.3g, of which saturates 13.6g; Cholesterol 208mg; Calcium 45mg; Fibre 4.2g; Sodium 183mg.

Hunter's chicken

This is a good simple chicken dish, for everyday eating. You may prefer to use skinless chicken for a lower fat meal, and replace the potato with pasta and a mixed pepper salad.

Serves four

30ml/2 tbsp olive oil
4 chicken portions, on the bone
1 large onion, thinly sliced
400g/14oz can chopped tomatoes
150ml/¼ pint/⅔ cup red wine
150ml/¼ pint/⅔ cup stock
1 garlic clove, crushed
1 rosemary sprig, finely chopped, plus extra
    whole sprigs to garnish
115g/4oz fresh field (portabello) mushrooms,
    thinly sliced
salt and ground black pepper

1 Heat the oil in a large, flameproof casserole until foaming. Add the chicken portions and fry for 5 minutes. Remove the chicken pieces and drain on kitchen paper.

2 Add the sliced onion and cook gently, stirring frequently, for about 3 minutes then stir in the tomatoes, red wine and stock. Add the crushed garlic and chopped rosemary and season. Bring to the boil, stirring continuously.

3 Return the chicken to the casserole and turn to coat with the sauce. Cover and simmer gently for 30 minutes.

4 Add the fresh mushrooms to the casserole and stir well to mix into the sauce. Continue simmering gently, uncovered, for 10 minutes, until the sauce has reduced. Taste and add more ground black pepper if necessary.

5 Garnish with the fresh rosemary sprigs, and serve immediately.

EAT WELL

In some instances, eating mashed potatoes can push up blood glucose levels too sharply; instead, try tossing boiled salad or new potatoes with a little olive oil and black pepper, then lightly crush them with a vegetable masher.

Energy 386kcal/1622kJ; Protein 53.6g; Carbohydrate 4.5g, of which sugars 4.1g; Fat 14.5g, of which saturates 4.5g; Cholesterol 155mg; Calcium 28mg; Fibre 1.5g; Sodium 141mg.

Chicken with summer vegetables

This is an all-in-the-pot dish, with the chicken providing the stock for the rest of the cooking and the sauce. Summer vegetables are wonderfully packed with flavour, and it is up to you to pick the selection you prefer: add canned beans for low GI carbohydrate and fibre.

Serves six

1.8kg/4lb boiling fowl (stewing chicken)
1 onion, peeled, studded with 6 cloves
1 bay leaf
a sprig each of thyme and parsley
10 black peppercorns
12 small potatoes, washed
8 small shallots, peeled
vegetables of your choice, including
   sugarsnap peas, carrots, courgettes
   (zucchini), broad (fava) beans and peas
2 x 400g/15oz cans flageolet beans
25g/1oz/2 tbsp butter
30ml/2 tbsp plain (all-purpose) flour
60ml/4 tbsp chopped fresh tarragon

1 Place the chicken in a large pan with the onion, bay leaf, thyme, parsley and peppercorns, with water to cover. Bring to the boil. Reduce the heat and simmer gently for 1½ hours. Skim off the froth, and add water if necessary.

2 Meanwhile prepare all the vegetables and place them in rows on a tray in order of cooking time, from the longest to the shortest.

3 Once cooked, remove the chicken from the pan and keep warm. Remove all the seasonings, either with a slotted spoon or by straining the mixture, then bring the cooking liquid back to the boil, skimming off any fat that may have appeared on the top.

4 Start to cook the vegetables in the liquid, putting the potatoes in first, then adding the shallots and carrots, if using, and finally the green vegetables that take no time at all – sugarsnap peas, for example, should go in when the potatoes are cooked. Add the flageolet beans for the final 5 minutes.

5 When the vegetables are cooked, place the chicken on a serving dish and surround with all the vegetables.

6 In a small pan melt the butter, add the flour and stir to create a roux. Slowly add some liquid from the large pan until a sauce is created – about 600ml/1 pint/2½ cups – and allow to simmer for a few minutes to reduce down and strengthen the flavour.

7 At the last moment stir in the chopped tarragon then ladle the sauce over the chicken and vegetables. Bring to the table and serve immediately.

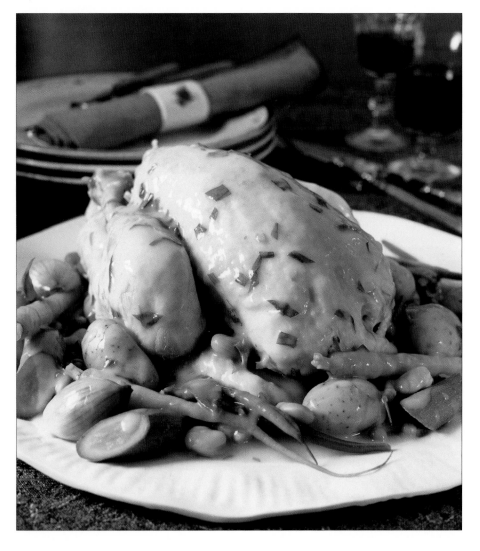

Energy 713kcal/2973kJ; Protein 51.2g; Carbohydrate 39.3g, of which sugars 13g; Fat 40g, of which saturates 12.9g; Cholesterol 261mg; Calcium 103mg; Fibre 5.4g; Sodium 250mg.

Pheasant with oatmeal herb stuffing

Game is a good source of low-fat protein. Pheasant is delicate and delicious with the richly flavoured herb stuffing. The traditional accompaniment is game chips and redcurrant sauce, but pasta or couscous and lots of barely cooked courgettes are just as good.

Serves four to six
2 oven-ready pheasants
6 unsmoked bacon rashers (strips)
30ml/2 tbsp olive oil
15g/½oz/2 tbsp seasoned flour
450ml/¾ pint/scant 2 cups
   chicken stock
salt and ground black pepper
watercress or rocket (arugula), to garnish

For the stuffing
1 small onion, finely chopped
225g/8oz chicken or pheasant livers, trimmed
   and finely chopped
115g/4oz/1 cup pinhead oatmeal
about 120ml/4fl oz/½ cup milk

1 To prepare the stuffing, put the onion and the pheasant livers into a mixing bowl with the oatmeal. Mix thoroughly and season with salt and pepper. Add enough milk to moisten slightly.

2 Preheat the oven to 200°C/400°F/ Gas 6. Wipe the birds inside and out and divide the stuffing between the two birds, spooning it in loosely to allow space for the oatmeal to expand.

3 Use cotton string to truss the pheasants for cooking, and lay the bacon rashers over the breasts.

4 Lay the birds in a roasting pan and drizzle the oil over them. Place in the oven and cook for 45–50 minutes, basting often.

5 Ten minutes before the end of the cooking time, remove the bacon rashers and set aside. Baste the birds and then dredge them with seasoned flour. Baste again and return to the oven to brown.

6 When cooked, remove the trussing strings and put the pheasants on to a heated serving dish. Keep warm, uncovered, while you make the gravy. Pour all but 30ml/2 tbsp of the fat out of the roasting pan.

7 Sprinkle the remaining flour into the roasting pan, stirring to blend and dislodge any sediment on the bottom.

8 Gradually blend in the stock, season and bring to the boil. Simmer for a few minutes, stirring, then pour into a heated sauceboat.

9 To serve, garnish the pheasant breasts with the bacon pieces and watercress or rocket. Hand the gravy round separately.

Energy 846kcal/3529kJ; Protein 69.7g; Carbohydrate 25.2g, of which sugars 1.1g; Fat 52.5g, of which saturates 23.1g; Cholesterol 598mg; Calcium 92mg; Fibre 2.3g; Sodium 697mg.

Venison pie

This is a modified version of shepherd's pie using rich yet lean venison. The mixed vegetable mash has a high GI value but including it with protein slows down digestion. Serve lots of green vegetables, such as kale or cabbage, and green beans, on the side.

Serves six

30ml/2 tbsp olive oil
3 leeks, washed, trimmed and chopped
1kg/2¼lb minced (ground) venison
30ml/2 tbsp chopped fresh parsley
300ml/½ pint/1¼ cups game consommé
salt and ground black pepper

For the topping
1.4kg/3¼lb mixed root vegetables, such as
  potatoes, sweet potatoes, parsnips and
  swede (rutabaga), coarsely chopped
15ml/1 tbsp horseradish sauce
30ml/2 tbsp olive oil

1 Heat the oil in a pan over a medium heat. Add the leeks and cook for about 8 minutes, or until they are softened and beginning to brown.

2 Add the minced venison to the pan and cook over a medium heat, stirring constantly, for about 10 minutes or until the venison is browned all over.

Cook's tips

This pie can be made with other minced (ground) meats, such as beef, lamb or pork, or a mixture of pork and beef. You may need to adapt the cooking times for these, but the basic recipe remains the same. You can also use other types of game, such as finely chopped or minced rabbit or hare.

3 Add the fresh parsley and stir it in thoroughly, then add the consommé and salt and ground black pepper. Stir well. Bring the mixture to the boil over a medium heat, then reduce the heat to low, cover and simmer for about 20 minutes, stirring occasionally.

4 Meanwhile, preheat the oven to 200°C/400°F/Gas 6 and prepare the pie topping. Cook the chopped root vegetables in boiling salted water to cover for 15–20 minutes.

5 Drain the vegetables and put them in a bowl. Mash them together with the horseradish sauce, olive oil and plenty of ground black pepper.

6 Spoon the venison mixture into a large ovenproof dish and cover the top evenly with the mashed vegetables.

7 Bake in the preheated oven for 20 minutes, or until piping hot and beginning to brown. Serve immediately, with steamed green vegetables.

EAT WELL

For a carbohydrate-packed mash that is not digested too speedily, combine crushed cooked lentils, chickpeas or butter (lima) beans with the vegetables. Red lentils are good with carrots, swedes (rutabaga), and sweet potatoes; try chickpeas or butter beans with potatoes. Olive oil is delicious with chives or parsley in mash.

Energy 307kcal/1291kJ; Protein 39.8g; Carbohydrate 13.2g, of which sugars 12.5g; Fat 12g, of which saturates 4.1g; Cholesterol 93mg; Calcium 154mg; Fibre 5.8g; Sodium 176mg.

Desserts, cakes and bakes

When you are thinking of a dessert, try and base it on a large proportion of fruit, which gives you a whole world of flavours, textures and colours to use in as many different cooking styles. Most fruit pudding recipes can be adapted to whatever fruit is in season. Desserts, cakes and cookies are often avoided by the health-conscious, but can actually make a useful contribution to good eating – dairy produce, nuts and wholegrains, as well as fruit, are important in a balanced diet. Whether you are making a dessert for a family meal, creating a tea-time treat or baking some bread, you will find the recipe in this chapter.

Apple and blackberry crumble

Fruit crumbles are an excellent choice for low-sugar desserts. Sweet dessert apples retain their shape during cooking or they can be stewed first for a soft result. Wholemeal flour and oatmeal help to balance the rate at which the sugar in the topping is digested.

Serves six to eight

900g/2lb sweet eating apples
450g/1lb/4 cups blackberries

For the topping
115g/4oz/½ cup butter
115g/4oz/1 cup wholemeal (whole-wheat) flour
50g/2oz/½ cup fine or medium
   pinhead oatmeal
30ml/2 tbsp soft light brown sugar
a little grated lemon rind (optional)

EAT WELL

Relying on naturally sweet flavours helps to cultivate a taste for less sweet dishes but sugar (for those who are not avoiding it) or sweetener can be added to individual portions at the table.

---

1 Preheat the oven to 200°C/400°F/ Gas 6. To make the crumble topping, rub the butter into the flour until it resembles fine breadcrumbs.

2 Add the oatmeal and brown sugar and continue to rub in until the mixture begins to stick together.

3 Mix the grated lemon rind, if using, in to the crumble mixture. Peel, core and slice the apples into wedges.

4 Put the apples, blackberries, lemon juice (if using), 30ml/2 tbsp water and the sugar into a shallow ovenproof dish, about 2 litres/3½ pints/9 cups capacity.

5 Cover the fruit with the topping. Sprinkle with a little cold water. Bake in the oven for 15 minutes, then reduce the heat to 190°C/375°F/Gas 5 and cook for another 15–20 minutes until crunchy and brown on top. Serve the crumble warm.

Energy 336kcal/1413kJ; Protein 4g; Carbohydrate 53.1g, of which sugars 30.8g; Fat 13.4g, of which saturates 6.8g; Cholesterol 27mg; Calcium 72mg; Fibre 3g; Sodium 81mg.

Summer fruit cobbler

This luscious dessert incorporates sweet strawberries and raspberries with low-fat curd cheese and a scone topping. Many other fruits can be used in this easy recipe; try plums, apricots or peaches. Served with yoghurt rather than custard it is the perfect finish to a Sunday lunch.

Serves four

450g/1lb/4 cups strawberries
250g/9oz/1½ cups raspberries
15ml/1 tbsp sugar, optional

For the scone topping
175g/6oz/1½ cups self-raising (self-rising) flour
5ml/1 tsp baking powder
15ml/1 tbsp soft light brown sugar
grated rind of 1 lemon
50g/2oz/¼ cup butter, melted
1 egg, beaten
250g/9oz low-fat curd (farmer's) cheese

1 Preheat the oven to 220°C/425°F/ Gas 7. Mix the fruit with the sugar, if using. Place in an ovenproof dish.

2 For the scone topping, combine the flour, baking powder and sugar in a large bowl together with the grated lemon rind, then add the melted butter and stir through. Add the beaten egg and mix thoroughly.

3 Dot spoonfuls of the curd cheese over the top of the fruit.

4 Place a scoop of the scone dough on top of each spoon of curd cheese. Bake for about 20 minutes. The curd cheese should be oozing out of the scone topping. Serve immediately.

EAT WELL
Scones and crumbles do not rely on sugar for success during baking. Getting used to eating desserts that are less sweet is important for good long-term blood glucose balance, with fewer fluctuations. Adding chopped dried fruit, such as apricots, adds natural sugar, which is all carbohydrate, but they are also full of nutrients and fibre, which also helps to slow down the sugar digestion.

Energy 385kcal/1615kJ; Protein 15.9g; Carbohydrate 46.3g, of which sugars 13.8g; Fat 17.3g, of which saturates 10.3g; Cholesterol 89mg; Calcium 257mg; Fibre 2.8g; Sodium 532mg.

Lemon and lime cheesecake

For special-occasion desserts, non-sugar sweeteners can be used in this type of uncooked recipe but it is best to avoid using them regularly. Alternatively, a small amount of sugar can be used but remember that the biscuit base is also sweetened.

Makes eight slices

150g/5oz/1½ cups digestive biscuits
  (graham crackers)
40g/1½oz/3 tbsp butter

For the topping
grated rind and juice of 2 lemons
10ml/2 tsp powdered gelatine
250g/9oz/generous 1 cup ricotta cheese
caster (superfine) sugar or sweetener, to taste
150ml/¼ pint/⅔ cup double (heavy) cream
2 eggs, separated

For the lime dressing
finely pared rind of 3 limes
150ml/¼ pint/⅔ cup unsweetened apple juice
5ml/1 tsp arrowroot mixed with a little water
a little green food colouring (optional)

1 Lightly grease a 20cm/8in round springform cake tin (pan). Place the biscuits in a food processor or blender and process until they form fine crumbs. Melt the butter in a large pan, then stir in the crumbs until well coated. Spoon into the prepared cake tin, press the crumbs down well in an even layer, then chill.

2 Make the topping. Place the lemon rind and juice in a pan and sprinkle over the gelatine. Leave for 5 minutes, then heat gently until the gelatine has melted. Set the mixture aside to cool slightly. Beat the ricotta cheese and sugar or sweetener in a bowl. Stir in the cream and egg yolks, then whisk in the cooled gelatine.

3 Whisk the egg whites in a grease-free bowl until they form soft peaks. Fold them into the cheese mixture. Spoon on to the biscuit base, level the surface and chill for 2–3 hours.

4 Meanwhile, make the lime dressing. Place the lime rind and apple juice in a small pan. Bring to the boil, stirring, then boil for 1 minute. Stir in the arrowroot mixture and continue to stir until the syrup boils again and thickens slightly. Remove from the heat immediately. Tint green with food colouring, if you like. Cool, then chill until required. Spoon the lime dressing over the set cheesecake. Remove from the tin and cut into slices to serve.

Energy 366kcal/1526kJ; Protein 6g; Carbohydrate 33.8g, of which sugars 23.5g; Fat 23.9g, of which saturates 13.8g; Cholesterol 105mg; Calcium 44mg; Fibre 0.4g; Sodium 166mg.

Tofu berry torte

This is a relatively low-sugar dessert, with the redcurrant jelly being the only source of refined sugar. Sugar in the fruit and apple juice sweetens the torte, while the low-fat tofu and yogurt make it deliciously creamy, a perfect foil to the summer fruit.

Serves six

425g/15oz firm tofu
300g/11oz natural (plain) yogurt
25ml/1½ tbsp/1½ sachets powdered gelatine
90ml/6 tbsp apple juice
175g/6oz/1¾ cups soft fruits, such as
    raspberries, strawberries and blueberries
30ml/2 tbsp redcurrant jelly
30ml/2 tbsp hot water

For the base
50g/2oz/¼ cup dairy-free, low-fat spread
    or margarine
30ml/2 tbsp apple juice
115g/4oz/6 cups unsweetened bran flakes

1 To make the base, place the low-fat spread or margarine and apple juice in a pan and heat them gently until the spread or margarine has melted. Crush the bran flakes and stir them into the apple juice mixture.

2 Tip the mixture into a 23cm/9in loose-based round flan tin (pan) and press down firmly with your fingers. Leave base to cool, then chill until set.

3 To make the filling, place the tofu and yogurt in a food processor and process them until smooth. Soak the gelatine in the apple juice, then heat to dissolve. Stir into the tofu mixture.

4 Spread the tofu mixture over the base, smoothing it evenly. Chill for 1–2 hours, until the filling has set.

EAT WELL
Made from soya beans, tofu is an excellent source of protein and it is low fat, making this dessert a well-balanced dish, with vitamins and health-giving nutrients in the fruit and fibre in the bran-flake base. It is useful for anyone allergic to dairy foods as a non-dairy cream or soya yogurt can be used instead of the ordinary yogurt.

5 Carefully remove the flan tin and place the cheesecake on a serving plate.

6 Arrange the soft fruits on top of the cheesecake. Place the redcurrant jelly in a small bowl and add the hot water. Stir well until the jelly has melted. Leave it to cool and then spoon or lightly brush it over the fruit to serve.

Energy 204kcal/854kJ; Protein 7.7g; Carbohydrate 23.2g, of which sugars 13.8g; Fat 9.5g, of which saturates 0.5g; Cholesterol 0mg; Calcium 311mg; Fibre 2.8g; Sodium 253mg.

Apple and bilberry fool

Mousses, creams and fools are easily adapted to reduce sugar quantities or omit them completely. Using dessert apples instead of cooking apples introduces a naturally sweet flavour and makes added sugar superfluous.

Serves six to eight

450g/1lb sweet dessert apples
450g/1lb/4 cups bilberries or blueberries
1 sachet powdered gelatine
2 egg whites
60ml/4 tbsp double (heavy) cream, to serve

1 Peel, core and slice the cooking apples, then put them into a large pan with the bilberries, 150ml/ ¼ pint/⅔ cup water and 75g/3oz/ scant ½ cup of the sugar. Cook gently for 15 minutes, until tender. Remove from the heat.

2 Strain the lemon juice into a cup, sprinkle the gelatine over and leave it to soak. When the gelatine has dissolved mix it into the fruit.

3 Turn the fruit mixture into a nylon sieve (strainer) over a large mixing bowl and press the fruit through it to make a purée; discard anything that is left in the sieve. Leave the purée to stand until it is cool and beginning to set.

4 Whisk the egg whites until they are standing in soft peaks.

EAT WELL
Remember that uncooked eggs are not recommended for anyone who is pregnant, elderly or unwell.

5 Using a metal spoon, fold the whites gently into the fruit purée to make a smooth mousse. Turn into serving glasses and chill until set. Serve topped with double cream.

Cook's tips
Bilberries grow prolifically in British moorland areas in late summer. This recipe stretches a modest amount of wild fruit. Blueberries are related and they work very well in this recipe. Yogurt can be substituted for cream.

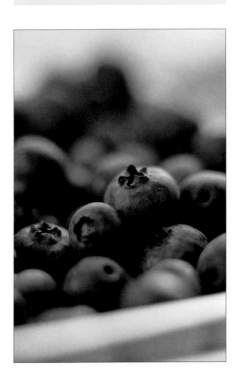

Energy 92kcal/385kJ; Protein 1.6g; Carbohydrate 13g, of which sugars 10.8g; Fat 4.1g, of which saturates 2.5g; Cholesterol 10mg; Calcium 6mg; Fibre 2g; Sodium 18mg.

Frozen melon

Artificial sweeteners do not work well in sorbets and ice creams, so these desserts should be reserved for small portions or rare treats. To extend a small portion of sweet sorbet, whizz it with yogurt in a food processor.

Serves 6
75ml/5 tbsp caster (superfine) sugar
15ml/1 tbsp lemon juice
60ml/4 tbsp water
1 medium cantaloupe melon or Charentais melon, about 1kg/2¼lb
crushed ice, cucumber slices and borage flowers, to decorate

1 Put the sugar, lemon juice and water in a heavy pan and heat gently until the sugar dissolves. Bring to the boil, and boil for 1 minute, without stirring, to make a syrup. Leave to cool.

4 If making by hand, pour the mixture into a plastic container and freeze for about 3–4 hours, beating twice with a fork or a whisk, or processing in a food processor, to break up the ice crystals and produce a smoother texture. If using an ice cream maker, churn the melon mixture until the sorbet holds its shape.

2 Cut the melon in half and discard the seeds. Carefully scoop out the flesh using a metal spoon or melon baller and place in a food processor, taking care to keep the halved shells intact.

3 Process the melon flesh until smooth, then transfer to a mixing bowl. Stir in the cooled sugar syrup and chill until very cold. Invert the melon shells and leave them to drain on kitchen paper, then transfer them to the freezer.

5 Remove the frozen melon shells from the freezer, pack the sorbet tightly into the melon shells and level the surface with a sharp knife.

6 Use a dessertspoon to scoop out the centre of each filled melon shell to simulate the seed cavity, then freeze the prepared fruit overnight until firm.

7 To serve, use a large knife to cut each melon half into three large wedges. Serve on a bed of crushed ice, either on a large platter or individual plates, and decorate with the cucumber slices and borage flowers.

Energy 67kcal/288kJ; Protein 0.6g; Carbohydrate 16.6g, of which sugars 16.6g; Fat 0.3g, of which saturates 0.1g; Cholesterol 0mg; Calcium 12mg; Fibre 0.1g; Sodium 3mg.

Peach and cardamom yogurt ice

Low-fat frozen desserts that rely on natural fruit for their sweetness make the perfect dessert for anyone with diabetes. This yogurt ice provides a useful source of calcium and vitamin C.

Serves four

8 cardamom pods
6 peaches, total weight about 500g/1¼lb,
    halved and stoned (pitted)
30ml/2 tbsp water
200ml/7fl oz/scant 1 cup bio natural
    (plain) yogurt

1 Put the cardamom pods on a board and crush them with the base of a ramekin, or use a mortar and pestle.

2 Chop the peaches and put them in a pan. Add the crushed cardamom pods, with their black seeds, and the measured water. Cover and simmer gently for about 10 minutes, or until the fruit is tender. Remove the pan from the heat and leave to cool.

3 Pour the peach mixture into a food processor or blender, process until smooth, then press through a sieve (strainer) placed over a bowl.

Cook's tip
Use bio natural (plain) yogurt for its extra mild taste. Greek (US strained plain) yogurt or ordinary natural yogurt are both much sharper, and tend to overwhelm the delicate taste of peach.

4 Add the yogurt to the purée and mix. Pour into a freezerproof tub and freeze for about 6 hours, beating once or twice with a whisk or in a food processor. To serve, scoop the ice cream on to a platter or into bowls.

EAT WELL
Try mango and strawberry instead of the peaches.

Energy 69kcal/296kJ; Protein 3.8g; Carbohydrate 13.3g, of which sugars 13.3g; Fat 0.6g, of which saturates 0.3g; Cholesterol 1mg; Calcium 104mg; Fibre 1.9g; Sodium 43mg.

Date and tofu ice

Generously spiced with cinnamon, this unusual ice cream is packed with soya protein and it contains no added sugar; it is also low in fat.

Serves four

250g/9oz/1½ cups stoned (pitted) dates
600ml/1 pint/2½ cups apple juice
5ml/1 tsp ground cinnamon
285g/10½oz pack chilled tofu, drained
   and cubed
150ml/¼ pint/⅔ cup unsweetened soya milk

1 Put the dates in a pan. Pour in 300ml/½ pint/1¼ cups of the apple juice and leave to soak for 2 hours. Simmer for 10 minutes, then leave to cool. Using a slotted spoon, lift out one-quarter of the dates, chop roughly and set aside.

2 Purée the remaining dates in a food processor or blender. Add the cinnamon and process with enough of the remaining apple juice to make a smooth paste.

3 Add the cubes of tofu to the food processor, a few at a time, processing after each addition. Finally, add the remaining apple juice and the soya milk and mix well to combine.

Cook's tip
You could make this tasty ice cream with any soft dried fruits; dried figs, apricots or peaches would be especially good. Alternatively you could use a combination for a vitamin- and fibre-packed feast.

4 Churn the mixture in an ice cream maker until very thick, but not thick enough to scoop. Scrape into a plastic tub.

5 Stir in most of the chopped dates, retaining a few pieces for garnishing, and freeze for 2–3 hours until firm.

6 Scoop into dessert glasses and decorate with the remaining chopped dates.

EAT WELL
Remember that dried fruits are naturally high in sugar and they can cause fluctuations in blood sugar levels. This tofu and date ice does not have added sugar and it can be served with fresh fruit or have fresh fruit mixed in at the last minute – try fresh strawberries, raspberries or cherries to bulk out the ice (making portions smaller and the sugar content less).

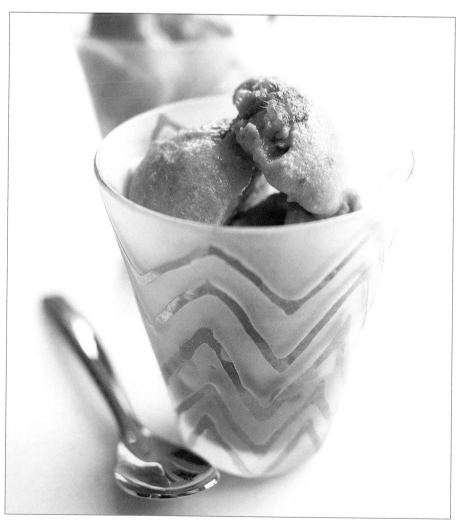

Energy 290kcal/1232kJ; Protein 9.1g; Carbohydrate 58.2g, of which sugars 57.9g; Fat 3.9g, of which saturates 0.5g; Cholesterol 0mg; Calcium 407mg; Fibre 2.5g; Sodium 24mg.

Mango and lime fool

Canned fruit is practical for everyday convenience, but this fool tastes even better if made with fresh fruit. This is an ideal dessert as it is naturally sweet and low in fat.

Serves four

400g/14oz can sliced mango
grated rind of 1 lime
juice of ½ lime
150ml/¼ pint/⅔ cup low-fat crème fraîche
90ml/6 tbsp low-fat Greek (US strained plain) yogurt
fresh mango slices, to decorate (optional)

1 Drain the mango slices and place them in the bowl of a food processor or in a blender. Add the grated lime rind and the freshly squeezed lime juice. Process or blend until the mixture forms a smooth mango purée.

2 Alternatively, mash the mango slices with a fork or a potato masher, then press the mixture through a sieve (strainer) with a wooden spoon until you achieve a smooth purée.

3 Pour the crème fraîche into a bowl and add the Greek yogurt.

4 Whisk the mixture with a balloon whisk until it is thick and then fold in the mango purée. Spoon the mango and lime fool into four small cups or glasses and chill for approximately 1–2 hours.

5 When serving, decorate each glass with fresh mango slices, if you like.

EAT WELL
Canned fruit in juice makes a good basis for a fruit salad, for example, pineapple pieces or peach slices are excellent with orange, apple and grapes. Serve fruit salads topped with roasted seeds (sunflower, sesame and pumpkin) with a dollop of yogurt for a great dessert or breakfast.

Energy 289kcal/1203kJ; Protein 2.4g; Carbohydrate 21.4g, of which sugars 21.3g; Fat 22.4g, of which saturates 13.7g; Cholesterol 51mg; Calcium 62mg; Fibre 0.7g; Sodium 27mg.

Rhubarb and ginger yogurt ice

Frozen yogurt flavoured with fruit makes a good alternative to very sweet, commercial ice cream. It is low in fat and high in calcium, which is essential for good bone health.

Serves six

300g/11oz/scant 1½ cups set bio natural (plain) live yogurt
200g/7oz/scant 1 cup mascarpone
350g/12oz/3 cups chopped rhubarb
30ml/2 tbsp clear honey
3 pieces preserved stem ginger, finely chopped

1 Whisk together the yogurt and mascarpone. Pour the mixture into a shallow freezerproof container and freeze for about 1 hour.

2 Put the rhubarb and honey in a pan and add 45ml/3 tbsp water. Cook over a very low heat, stirring occasionally, for 15 minutes, or until the rhubarb is soft. Remove the pan from the heat and set aside to cool. When the fruit has cooled, place it in a food processor or blender and process to a purée.

3 Remove the semi-frozen yogurt mixture from the freezer and fold in the rhubarb purée. Beat well until smooth, breaking up the ice crystals, then fold in the chopped ginger.

4 Return the yogurt ice to the freezer and freeze for 2 hours. Remove from the freezer and beat again, then freeze until solid. To serve, scoop the yogurt ice into individual serving bowls.

EAT WELL
The problem with ices is that they need a lot of sugar (or fat, or both) to soften their set. Preserved stem ginger in syrup is sweet and sugar-rich, so for an alternative, omit the stem ginger and add a large knob of peeled chopped fresh ginger.

Energy 106kcal/446kJ; Protein 6.2g; Carbohydrate 9.1g, of which sugars 9.1g; Fat 5.4g, of which saturates 3.3g; Cholesterol 15mg; Calcium 150mg; Fibre 0.8g; Sodium 44mg.

Courgette and ginger cake

Whisked sponges require less sugar in the baking process than creamed-fat mixtures – here the mixture is adapted into a spicy teabread in this light recipe.

Serves eight to ten

3 eggs
60ml/4 tbsp caster (superfine) sugar
120ml/4fl oz/½ cup sunflower oil
5ml/1 tsp vanilla extract
225g/8oz courgettes (zucchini), grated
5cm/2in piece fresh root ginger, peeled
    and grated
350g/12oz/3 cups unbleached plain
    (all-purpose) flour
5ml/1 tsp baking powder
pinch of salt
5ml/1 tsp ground cinnamon
1 piece stem ginger, chopped
15ml/1 tbsp demerara sugar

1 Preheat the oven to 190ºC/325ºF/ Gas 5. Whisk the eggs and sugar until creamy. Slowly beat in the oil until the mixture forms a batter. Mix in the vanilla extract, then add the grated courgettes and fresh ginger.

2 Sift together the flour, baking powder and salt into a large bowl. Add the cinnamon and mix, then stir the dried ingredients into the courgette mixture.

3 Lightly grease a 900g/2lb loaf tin and pour in the courgette mixture. Smooth and level the top, then sprinkle the chopped ginger and demerara sugar over the surface.

4 Bake for 1 hour until a skewer inserted into the centre comes out clean. Leave the cake in the tin to cool for about 20 minutes, then turn out on to a wire rack.

EAT WELL
Courgettes (zucchini) make moist cakes, contributing vegetable goodness to semi-sweet mixtures. Select firm young courgettes, trim off the ends and leave the nutritious skin on for added colour.

Energy 252kcal/1060kJ; Protein 5.6g; Carbohydrate 35.6g, of which sugars 8.8g; Fat 10.7g, of which saturates 1.6g; Cholesterol 57mg; Calcium 73mg; Fibre 1.3g; Sodium 82mg.

Chocolate and prune cake

Thanks to gram flour, this delicious cake is high in soluble fibre but it is also quite high in sugar from the prunes, so enjoy it as an occasional treat.

Makes a 20cm/8in cake

300g/11oz dark (bittersweet) chocolate
150g/5oz/²/₃ cup low-fat spread
200g/7oz/generous 1 cup ready-to-eat stoned
   (pitted) prunes, quartered
3 eggs, beaten
150g/5oz/1¼ cups gram flour, sifted with
   10ml/2 tsp baking powder
120ml/4fl oz/¼ cup soya milk

1 Preheat the oven to 180°C/350°F/ Gas 4. Grease and base-line a deep 20cm/8in round cake tin (pan). Melt the chocolate in a heatproof bowl over a pan of hot water.

2 Mix the low-fat spread and prunes in a food processor. Process until light and fluffy, then scrape into a bowl.

Cook's tips

Use dark (bittersweet) chocolate with a high proportion of cocoa solids (70 per cent). You can substitute ready-to-eat apricots in place of the prunes, if you wish.

3 Gradually fold in the melted chocolate and eggs, alternately with the flour mixture. Beat in the soya milk.

4 Spoon the mixture into the cake tin, level the surface with a spoon, then bake for 20–30 minutes or until the cake is firm to the touch. A fine skewer inserted in the cake should come out clean. Leave to cool on a wire rack.

EAT WELL
Chickpea flour or besan can be used instead of gram flour – both contribute protein and fibre.

Energy 3173kcal/13294kJ; Protein 65g; Carbohydrate 376.8g, of which sugars 259.8g; Fat 166.1g, of which saturates 72.6g; Cholesterol 598mg; Calcium 537mg; Fibre 23.6g; Sodium 1268mg.

Chunky chocolate and banana muffins

American muffins are simple and quick to make and they work well with less sugar than usual. Serve warm while the chocolate is still gooey.

Makes twelve

90ml/6 tbsp milk
2 eggs
150g/5oz/10 tbsp unsalted butter, melted
225g/8oz/2 cups unbleached plain
  (all-purpose) flour
pinch of salt
5ml/1 tsp baking powder
30ml/2 tbsp golden caster (superfine) sugar
105g/4oz plain (semisweet) chocolate
2 small firm bananas, mashed

1 Place 12 large paper muffin cases in a deep muffin tin (pan). Preheat the oven to 200°C/400°F/Gas 6.

2 Whisk together the milk, eggs and butter in a bowl until combined.

3 Sift together the flour, salt and baking powder into a separate bowl. Chop the chocolate into small pieces, add to the flour mixture together with the sugar and then stir to combine.

4 Slowly stir in the milk mixture, but do not beat it. Gently fold in the mashed bananas.

5 Spoon the mixture into the paper cases. Bake for 20 minutes until golden. Cool on a wire rack.

Apricot and hazelnut oat cookies

These cookies have a lovely chewy texture. Any combination of dried fruit and nuts can be used.

Makes nine

115g/4oz/½ cup unsalted butter, plus extra
  for greasing
30ml/2 tbsp golden caster (superfine) sugar
30ml/2 tbsp orange juice
115g/4oz/1 cup self-raising (self-rising)
  flour, sifted
115g/4oz/1 cup rolled oats
75g/3oz/scant ½ cup ready-to-eat dried
  apricots, chopped

For the topping
25g/1oz/2 tbsp ready-to-eat dried
  apricots, chopped
25g/1oz/¼ cup hazelnuts, toasted

> **EAT WELL**
> Oats provide soluble fibre, which is helpful for regulating blood glucose and cholesterol levels.

1 Spread the nuts on a baking tray and place under a grill (broiler) until toasted. You could also do this in a frying pan or in the oven. Chop when cool.

2 Preheat the oven to 170°C/325°F/ Gas 3. Lightly grease a large baking sheet. Put the butter, sugar and orange juice in a small heavy pan and cook over a gentle heat, until the butter has melted and the sugar has dissolved, stirring occasionally. Remove the pan from the heat.

3 Put the flour, oats and apricots in a bowl, add the butter mixture and mix with a wooden spoon to form a sticky dough. Divide the dough into nine pieces and place on the baking sheet. Press into 1cm/½in thick rounds. Scatter over the apricots and hazelnuts and press into the dough.

4 Bake for 15 minutes until golden and slightly crisp. Leave to cool on the baking sheet for 5 minutes, then transfer to a wire rack.

Energy 240kcal/1003kJ; Protein 3.7g; Carbohydrate 26.3g, of which sugars 11.6g; Fat 14.1g, of which saturates 8.4g; Cholesterol 59mg; Calcium 47mg; Fibre 1g; Sodium 92mg.
Energy 262kcal/1098kJ; Protein 3.7g; Carbohydrate 33.2g, of which sugars 14.4g; Fat 13.6g, of which saturates 6.8g; Cholesterol 27mg; Calcium 71mg; Fibre 2.1g; Sodium 130mg.

Iced carob cookies

These heavenly cookies, with their creamy topping, are made with wholemeal flour and rolled oats, with a relatively modest amount of sugar.

Makes twelve to sixteen

115g/4oz/½ cup butter
10ml/2 tsp carob powder
115g/4oz/1 cup wholemeal (whole-wheat) flour
5ml/1 tsp baking powder
45ml/3 tbsp muscovado (molasses) sugar
50g/2oz/generous ½ cup rolled oats

For the topping
50g/2oz carob bar, coarsely chopped
45ml/3 tbsp double (heavy) cream
15ml/1 tbsp chopped ready-to-eat dried apricots

1 Preheat the oven to 190°C/375°F/ Gas 5.

2 Put the butter in a large pan and add the carob powder. Stir over a low heat until the mixture is smooth and combined. Stir in the remaining ingredients and mix well.

3 Line the base and sides of an 18cm/7in square shallow cake tin (pan) with baking parchment.

4 Press the mixture into the prepared tin and bake for about 20–25 minutes until just set. Mark into squares or bars while still hot. Leave to cool in the tin.

5 To make the topping, stir the carob and cream in a small pan over a low heat. Spread over the cookies and sprinkle the apricots on top.

Energy 133kcal/554kJ; Protein 1.7g; Carbohydrate 12.3g, of which sugars 5.5g; Fat 8.9g, of which saturates 5.3g; Cholesterol 19mg; Calcium 11mg; Fibre 1.1g; Sodium 52mg.

Lemon shortbread

This shortbread recipe has slightly less sugar than usual, which is lower than most sweet biscuits, but it is high in fat, so is best reserved for an occasional indulgence.

Makes about 48 fingers

275g/10oz/2½ cups plain (all-purpose) or wholemeal (whole-wheat) flour
50g/2oz/½ cup ground almonds
175g/6oz/¾ cup butter, softened
60ml/4 tbsp caster (superfine) sugar
grated rind of 1 lemon

1 Preheat the oven to 180°C/350°F/ Gas 4 and oil a large Swiss roll tin (jelly roll pan) or baking tray.

2 To make in a food processor: put the flour, ground almonds, softened butter, caster sugar and lemon rind into the food processor and process until the mixture comes together. (To make by hand, see right.)

3 Place the mixture in the tin and flatten it out. Bake in the preheated oven for 20 minutes, or until pale golden brown.

Eat well
Using wholemeal flour gives added fibre. Reduce the sugar if you want.

4 Remove from the oven and immediately mark the shortbread into fingers or squares while the mixture is soft. Allow to cool a little, and then transfer to a wire rack and leave until cool before storing, although it is delicious eaten when still warm from the oven. If stored in an airtight container, the shortbread should keep for up to two weeks.

To make by hand Sift the flour and almonds on to a pastry board or work surface. Cream the butter and sugar together in a mixing bowl, until it is soft and light. Turn the creamed mixture on to the flour and almonds and work it together by hand to make a smooth dough. Continue as from step 3.

Energy 57kcal/239kJ; Protein 0.8g; Carbohydrate 5.6g, of which sugars 1.2g; Fat 3.7g, of which saturates 2g; Cholesterol 8mg; Calcium 12mg; Fibre 0.3g; Sodium 22mg.

Oatmeal biscuits

Although not as neat as bought ones, these unsweetened home-made oatmeal biscuits make up in flavour and interest anything they might lose in presentation. Serve them with full-flavoured cheeses instead of commercial crackers, and carry them with you for instant snacks.

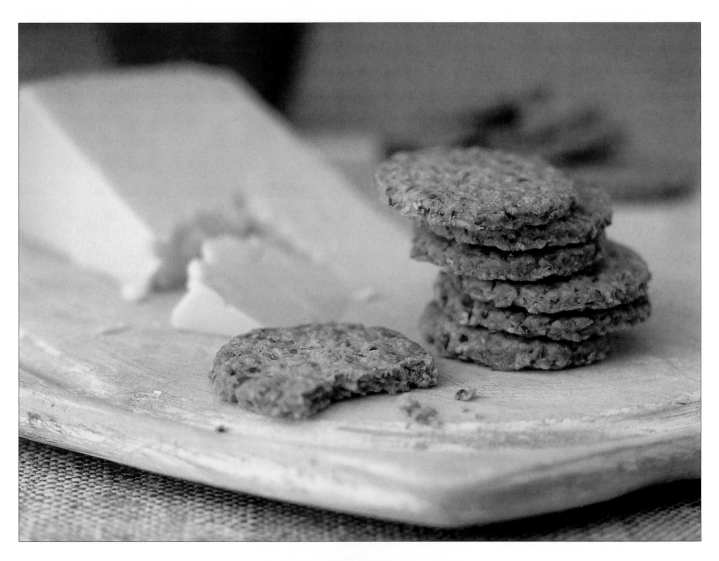

Makes about eighteen

75g/3oz/⅔ cup plain (all-purpose) flour
2.5ml/½ tsp salt
1.5ml/¼ tsp baking powder
115g/4oz/1 cup fine pinhead oatmeal
65g/2½oz/generous ¼ cup butter

1 Preheat the oven to 200°C/400°F/ Gas 6 and grease a baking sheet.

2 Sift the flour, salt and baking powder into a mixing bowl. Add the oatmeal and mix well. Rub in the fat to make a crumbly mixture, then blend in enough water to make a stiff dough.

3 Turn on to a worktop sprinkled with fine oatmeal and knead until smooth and manageable. Roll out to about 3mm/⅛in thick and cut into rounds, squares or triangles. Place on the baking sheet.

4 Bake in the preheated oven for about 15 minutes, until crisp. Cool the biscuits on a wire rack.

5 When cold, store the biscuits in an airtight container lined with baking parchment. Check for crispness before serving; reheat for 4–5 minutes at 200°C/400°F/Gas 6 to crisp.

Cook's tip
Spread with low-fat soft cheese and top with sweet dessert apple for a quick but healthy snack.

Energy 67kcal/279kJ; Protein 1.2g; Carbohydrate 7.9g, of which sugars 0.1g; Fat 3.6g, of which saturates 1.3g; Cholesterol 1mg; Calcium 10mg; Fibre 0.6g; Sodium 31mg.

Drop scones

These light drop scones make a quick and easy breakfast, elevenses or teatime snack served with butter and traditionally drizzled with honey, although this is of course optional. You could also eat them with a white crumbly cheese, such as Wensleydale or Cheshire.

Makes eight to ten

115g/4oz/1 cup plain (all-purpose) flour
5ml/1 tsp bicarbonate of soda (baking soda)
5ml/1 tsp cream of tartar
25g/1oz/2 tbsp butter, diced
1 egg, beaten
about 150ml/¼ pint/⅔ cup milk

1 Sift the flour, bicarbonate of soda and cream of tartar together into a mixing bowl. Add the diced butter and rub it into the flour with your fingertips until the mixture resembles fine, evenly textured breadcrumbs.

2 Lightly grease a griddle pan or heavy frying pan, then preheat it. Make a well in the centre of the flour mixture, then stir in the egg. Add the milk a little at a time, stirring it in to check consistency.

3 When you have added enough milk to give a thick creamy consistency, cook the scones in batches. Drop three or four evenly sized spoonfuls of the mixture, spaced slightly apart, on the griddle or frying pan. Cook over a medium heat for 2–3 minutes, until bubbles rise to the surface and burst.

4 Turn the scones over and cook for a further 2–3 minutes. Place the cooked scones between the folds of a clean dish towel while cooking to keep warm. Serve with butter and honey.

Cook's tip
Placing the cooked scones in a clean, folded dish towel keeps them warm, soft and moist. Bring to the table like this and ask your guests to pull them out.

EAT WELL
For a dessert top the scones with fruit and low-fat soft cheese. Try fresh berries or diced mango, or cook sliced dessert apple in a little butter in a frying pan until browned.

Energy 59kcal/249kJ; Protein 2g; Carbohydrate 10.9g, of which sugars 1.8g; Fat 1.1g, of which saturates 0.2g; Cholesterol 11mg; Calcium 65mg; Fibre 0.4g; Sodium 56mg.

Chelsea buns

Chelsea buns are said to have been invented in London at the end of the 17th century. They make a good between-meals snack, as an occasional treat.

Makes twelve buns

500g/1¹/₄lb/4¹/₂ cups unbleached strong white bread flour
2.5ml/¹/₂ tsp salt
50g/2oz/¹/₄ cup butter, softened
5ml/1 tsp fast action, easy-blend dried yeast
225ml/8fl oz/scant 1 cup hand-hot milk
1 egg, beaten

For the filling
25g/1oz/2 tbsp butter, melted
115g/4oz/²/₃ cup sultanas (golden raisins)
25g/1oz/3 tbsp mixed chopped (candied) peel
25g/1oz/2 tbsp currants
5ml/1 tsp mixed (apple pie) spice

For the glaze
50g/2oz/2oz/¹/₄ cup caster (superfine) sugar
60ml/4 tbsp water
5ml/1 tsp orange flower water

1 Place the flour in a bowl. Add the salt and then rub in the butter. Stir in the yeast. Make a well in the middle of the dry ingredients. Pour the milk into the bowl and stir in some of the flour mixture, then add the egg and mix everything to a firm dough.

2 Turn the dough out on to a floured surface and knead it thoroughly for about 10 minutes, until it is smooth and elastic.

3 Roll out the dough to form a square that is approximately 30cm/12in, and brush with melted butter.

4 Sprinkle the buttered dough with the sultanas, mixed peel, currants and mixed spice, leaving a 1cm/¹/₂in border along one edge. Starting at a covered edge, roll the dough up. Press the edges together to seal.

5 Lightly grease a 23cm/9in square cake tin (pan). Cut the roll into 12 slices and then place these cut sides uppermost in the prepared tin.

6 Cover with oiled clear film (plastic wrap). Leave to rise in a warm place for about 1 hour, or until the buns have doubled in size. Meanwhile, preheat the oven to 200°C/400°F/Gas 6.

7 Bake the buns for 15–20 minutes, or until they have risen well and are evenly golden all over. Once they are baked, leave them to cool slightly in the tin before turning them out on to a wire rack to cool further.

8 Make the glaze. Mix the caster sugar and water in a small pan. Heat, stirring occasionally, until the sugar is completely dissolved. Then boil the mixture rapidly for 1–2 minutes without stirring, until syrupy.

9 Stir the orange flower water into the glaze and then brush the mixture over the warm buns. Serve the Chelsea buns when they are still fresh, they are delicious when still slightly warm.

Energy 287kcal/1208kJ; Protein 6.1g; Carbohydrate 43.5g, of which sugars 16.6g; Fat 11.1g, of which saturates 2.3g; Cholesterol 26mg; Calcium 85mg; Fibre 1.3g; Sodium 243mg.

Barley bannocks

Bannocks are Scottish, but similar cakes or breads were made in most Northern European countries. They were traditionally cooked on a griddle on top of a stove or open fire, but baking them in the oven works very well. They make an excellent source of slow-release carbohydrate.

Serves six

225g/8oz/2 cups barley flour
50g/2oz/½ cup plain (all-purpose) flour
5ml/1 tsp cream of tartar
2.5ml/½ tsp salt
5ml/1 tsp bicarbonate of soda (baking soda)
250ml/8fl oz/1 cup buttermilk or natural
(plain) yogurt

1 Preheat the oven to 180°C/350°F/ Gas 4. Mix the barley flour, the plain flour, cream of tartar and salt together in a bowl.

2 Mix the bicarbonate of soda with the buttermilk or yogurt then pour this mixture into the dry ingredients. Mix to a soft dough like a scone mix.

3 Turn the dough out on to a floured surface and press down with your hands to make the whole dough, about 1cm/½in thick.

4 Cut the dough into six segments and place on an oiled baking sheet. Bake in the oven for about 15 minutes.

> **EAT WELL**
> Yeast-free breads of this type are easy to make and freeze well.

Energy 344kcal/1452kJ; Protein 10.4g; Carbohydrate 54.6g, of which sugars 4.8g; Fat 11g, of which saturates 6.1g; Cholesterol 27mg; Calcium 157mg; Fibre 8.4g; Sodium 552mg.

Wholemeal soda bread

Soda bread is best eaten on the day of baking, but it slices better if left to cool and "set" for a few hours. It freezes well, either whole or cut into chunks, ready for a quick snack with cheese and celery or a bowl of home-made soup.

Makes one loaf

450g/1lb/4 cups wholemeal
   (whole-wheat) flour
175g/6oz/1½ cups plain (all-purpose) flour
7.5ml/1½ tsp bicarbonate of soda
   (baking soda)
5ml/1 tsp salt
about 450ml/¾ pint/scant 2 cups buttermilk

1 Preheat the oven to 200°C/400°F/ Gas 6, and grease a baking sheet. Combine the dry ingredients in a mixing bowl and stir in enough buttermilk to make a fairly soft dough. Turn on to a work surface dusted with wholemeal flour and knead lightly until smooth.

EAT WELL

Use the basic wholemeal (whole-wheat) soda bread recipe as a basis for making semi-sweet fruit loaves. Add raisins or mixed dried fruit; or try chopped ready-to-eat dried apricots or dates. Chopped nuts are good, as are lightly roasted sunflower, sesame and pumpkin seeds. For savoury nutty or seeded breads, chopped fresh herbs go well.

The chemical reaction that the heat of the oven causes in the buttermilk is what makes the bread rise. It is important that as soon as it is ready, the dough is placed in a hot oven straight away before the gases escape.

2 Form the dough into a circle, about 4cm/1½in thick. Lay on the baking sheet and mark a deep cross in the top with a floured knife.

3 Bake for about 45 minutes, or until the bread is browned and sounds hollow when tapped on the base. Cool on a wire rack. If a soft crust is preferred, wrap the loaf in a clean dish towel while cooling.

Cook's tip

Instead of buttermilk, mix the same amount of fresh milk with the juice of half a lemon to create the same chemical reaction.

Energy 2264kcal/9627kJ; Protein 74.5g; Carbohydrate 502g, of which sugars 30.5g; Fat 9.5g, of which saturates 1.9g; Cholesterol 18mg; Calcium 1454mg; Fibre 19.2g; Sodium 2933mg.

Muesli and date bread

This loaf is a good example of how home baking allows you to make low-GI breads with less salt than shop-bought bread. Use homemade, unsweetened muesli for best results.

Makes one loaf

75g/3oz/³/₄ cup strong wholemeal (whole-wheat) bread flour
300g/10¹/₂oz/2²/₃ cups unbleached white bread flour
2.5ml/¹/₂ tsp salt
45ml/3 tbsp skimmed milk powder (non fat dry milk)
7.5ml/1¹/₂ tsp fast action, easy-blend dried yeast
150g/5¹/₂oz/generous 1¹/₂ cups unsweetened fruit and nut muesli
65g/2¹/₂oz/scant ¹/₂ cup dates, chopped
260ml/9fl oz/scant 1¹/₈ cups hand hot water
30ml/2 tbsp sunflower oil
15ml/1 tbsp clear honey

1 Mix the wholemeal flour and white flour in a bowl with the salt, milk powder and yeast. Stir in the muesli and dates, make a well in the middle and pour in the water, oil and honey.

2 Mix the dry ingredients and liquid to make a firm dough. Turn this dough out on to a floured surface and knead it thoroughly for about 10 minutes, until it is smooth and elastic. Lightly oil a baking sheet.

3 Shape the dough into a plump round and place it on the prepared baking sheet. Using a sharp knife make three cuts on the top about 1cm/¹/₂in deep, to divide the bread into six sections.

4 Cover the loaf with lightly oiled clear film and leave to rise for about an hour, or until it has almost doubled in size.

5 Preheat the oven to 200°C/400°F/Gas 6. Bake the loaf for 30–35 minutes until it is golden and hollow sounding when tapped underneath. Transfer it to a wire rack to cool.

EAT WELL
Baking your own bread is very satisfying, and means you are in total control of the salt and sugar levels of your loaves. If you don't have the time to hand bake, consider buying a bread machine.

Barley-enriched farmhouse loaf

Barley adds a very distinctive, earthy, slightly nutty flavour to this crusty loaf and it also helps to lower the GI value of a standard white loaf.

Makes one loaf

400g/14oz/3¹/₂ cups strong unbleached white bread flour
115g/4oz/1 cup barley flour
5ml/1 tsp salt
7.5ml/1¹/₂ tsp easy-blend dried yeast
10ml/2 tsp sugar
200g/7fl oz/1¹/₈ cups hand-hot water
100ml/31/2fl oz/¹/₂ cup hand-hot milk
25g/1oz/2 tbsp pumpkin or sunflower seeds
flour, for dusting

1 Mix the white and barley flours in a bowl. Stir in the salt, yeast and sugar, then make a well in the centre. Pour in the water and milk, and mix the ingredients to a firm dough.

2 Turn the dough out on to a floured surface and knead it for about 10 minutes, until it is smooth and elastic. Knead the seeds in to the dough.

3 Lightly oil a 900g/2lb loaf tin (pan) measuring 18.5 x 12cm/7¹/₄ x 4¹/₂in. Shape the dough into a rectangle the same length as the tin.

4 Roll up the dough lengthwise, tuck the ends under, and place in the tin with the seam underneath. Cover with lightly oiled clear film (plastic wrap). Leave to rise for 1 hour until the dough reaches the top of the tin. Preheat the oven to 220°C/425°F/Gas 7.

5 Dust the top of the loaf with flour, and make a deep lengthways cut along the top. Leave to rest for 10 minutes. Bake for 15 minutes, reduce the oven to 200°C/400°F/Gas 6 and bake for 20–25 minutes more, until the bread sounds hollow when tapped on the base. Cool on a wire rack.

Energy 2283kcal/9675kJ; Protein 70.8g; Carbs 437.3g, of which sugars 85.2g; Fat 39.6g, of which saturates 5.9g; Cholesterol 5mg; Calcium 1111mg; Fibre 28.6g; Sodium 335mg.
Energy 2009kcal/8531kJ; Protein 55.1g; Carbohydrate 426.7g, of which sugars 21.6g; Fat 20.7g, of which saturates 3g; Cholesterol 6mg; Calcium 737mg; Fibre 13.9g; Sodium 2025mg.

Chickpea and peppercorn bread

Bread may be a basic food, but it certainly isn't boring, as this exciting combination proves. Chickpeas add flavour, moisture and slow-release carbohydrate.

Makes one loaf

500g/1lb 2oz/4¹/₂ cups strong unbleached white bread flour
10ml/2 tsp drained fresh pink peppercorns in brine
10ml/2 tsp drained fresh green peppercorns in brine
22ml/1¹/₂ tbsp skimmed milk powder (non fat dry milk)
5 ml/1 tsp salt
10ml/2 tsp sugar
7.5ml/1¹/₂ tsp easy-blend, fast-action dried yeast
175g/6oz/1 cup canned chickpeas
250ml/9fl oz/generous 1 cup hand-hot water
30ml/2 tbsp extra virgin olive oil
milk, for brushing (optional)

1 Mash the chickpeas with a fork so that they are well crushed. You can also do this in a food processor, but don't over-process to a paste.

2 In a large bowl, mix the flour, both types of peppercorn, milk powder, sugar and yeast. Make a well in the middle of the ingredients.

3 Add the crushed chickpeas to the flour mixture, then pour in the water and olive oil. Mix all the ingredients to form a stiff dough.

4 Turn the dough on to a floured work surface and knead thoroughly, for about 10 minutes, until smooth and elastic.

5 Lightly oil a 900g/2lb loaf tin (pan) measuring 18.5 x 12cm/7¹/₄ x 4¹/₂in. Shape the dough to fit in the tin, the cover loosely with oiled clear film (plastic wrap).

6 Leave the dough in a warm place for 1¹/₂-2 hours, until the dough has doubled in size. Preheat the oven to 220°C/425°F/Gas 7.

7 Bake for 15 minutes, then reduce the oven to 200°C/400°F/Gas 6 and bake for a further 20–25 minutes until the bread is golden and sounds hollow when turned out and tapped on the base. Cool on a wire rack.

Energy 2220kcal/9410kJ; Protein 67.6g; Carbohydrate 438.8g, of which sugars 30.3g; Fat 33.7g, of which saturates 4.8g; Cholesterol 3mg; Calcium 1062mg; Fibre 22.7g; Sodium 2487mg.

Courgette and three-seed bread

The grated courgette combines with the flour during kneading to make a moist succulent bread. The proportion of wholemeal flour, together with the seeds, adds texture and flavour.

Makes one loaf

375g/13oz/3¼ cups strong unbleached white
   bread flour
75g/3oz/¾ cup strong wholemeal (whole-
   wheat) bread flour
40g/1½oz/3 tbsp butter
22ml/1½ tbsp sunflower seeds
22ml/1½ tbsp pumpkin seeds
10ml/2 tsp millet seeds
7.5ml/1½ tsp salt
7.5ml/1½ tsp sugar
7.5ml/1½ tsp easy-blend (rapid-rise)
   dried yeast
175g/6oz/1 cup grated courgette (zucchini)
75ml/5 tbsp buttermilk
55ml/2fl oz/¼ cup water
cornmeal, for sprinkling

1 Mix the white and wholemeal flours in a bowl. Rub in the butter and then mix in the sunflower, pumpkin and millet seeds, with the salt, sugar and yeast. Make a well in the middle.

2 Add the courgette and buttermilk, then pour in the water. Mix in the dry ingredients to form a stiff dough. Turn out the dough on to a floured surface and knead it thoroughly, for about 10 minutes, until it is smooth and elastic.

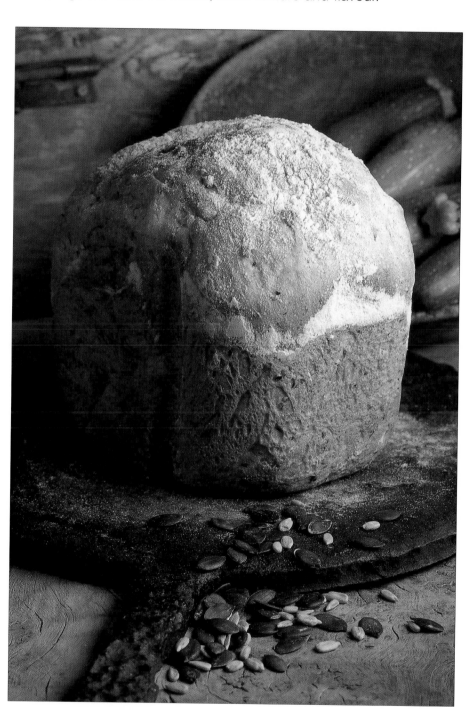

3 Lightly oil a 900g/2lb loaf tin (pan) measuring measuring 18.5 x 12cm/ 7¼ x 4½in. Shape the dough to fit in the tin, then cover loosely with oiled clear film (plastic wrap).

4 Leave to rise in a warm place for about 1½-2 hours until doubled in size.

5 Preheat the oven to 220°C/425°F/ Gas 7. Bake the loaf for 15 minutes. then reduce the oven to 200°C/400°F/ Gas 6 and bake the bread for a further 25–30 minutes until the bread is well browned and sounds hollow when turned out and tapped on the base. Cool on a wire rack.

Energy 2185kcal/9216kJ; Protein 60g; Carbohydrate 369.6g, of which sugars 22.3g; Fat 61.4g, of which saturates 24.1g; Cholesterol 88mg; Calcium 752mg; Fibre 22.6g; Sodium 2025mg.

Index